Terence Blacker is the author of five novels, the most recent of which is *The Twyning*, and of the acclaimed biography of Willie Donaldson, *You Cannot Live as I Have Lived and Not End Up Like This*. He writes a weekly column for the *Independent*.

A Regal Correspondence

First published in 2013 by
HEADLINE PUBLISHING GROUP

First published in paperback in 2014 by
HEADLINE PUBLISHING GROUP

1

Cataloguing in Publication Data is available from the British Library

Paperback ISBN 978 0 7553 6582 1

Typeset in Trump Medieval by Avon DataSet Ltd,
Bidford-on-Avon, Warwickshire

Printed and bound in Great Britain by Clays Ltd, St Ives plc

HEADLINE PUBLISHING GROUP
An Hachette UK Company
338 Euston Road
London NW1 3BH

www.headline.co.uk
www.hachette.co.uk
www.andyseed.co.uk

BUCKINGHAM PALACE
20.7.13
SW1A 1AA

Yours, E.R.

A Regal Correspondence

headline

Foreword

For some forty years of my professional life, it was my privilege to serve in the Royal Household of Her Majesty the Queen. I was, from 1983 until my retirement in 1996, senior personal adviser to the Private Secretary, acting essentially as a conduit between the press office, Whitehall and Her Majesty.

When I retired, the Queen did me the honour of requesting that I should continue my contact with the private office by writing her a weekly digest of the week's news, now known in the private office as 'the Bulletin', and enclosing any press cuttings that I felt Her Majesty might find interesting, useful or, occasionally, amusing.

Quite soon, she acquired the habit of replying to the Bulletin, giving her own perspective on current events, and over time these missives became relaxed and even personal in tone. A relationship of trust had developed between us when I worked at the palace, and perhaps now, surrounded by formality and constrained as to the opinions she could express, she found some small relief in being able to write openly and frankly to a contemporary (I am a year older than Her Majesty) who understood her life better than most and was reliably discreet.

I confess it was something of a surprise last year when, for reasons that are touched upon in the following pages, the Queen expressed the wish that some of these letters, covering the twelve months between the London Olympics and the birth of Prince George, should be made available to a wider, public readership.

Compiling and ordering those letters has been the most agreeable of duties. The Queen, while laying no claim to be a *belle lettriste*, writes clearly and directly in her unmistakeable, bold handwriting. The letters that follow are, apart from a small number of omissions made for legal or security reasons, as she wrote them to me to be delivered every week without fail to my flat in Pimlico.

Perusing them when they arrived on those Tuesday mornings afforded me the greatest pleasure, and I trust that this collection will be similarly rewarding to those, in whatever walk of life, who read them here.

Sir Jeremy Scrimgeour GCB GCVO
August 2013

Dear Sir Jeremy

What a joy it was to read your Bulletin at the end of a somewhat strenuous week. Of course, one knew that having the Olympics in London ('hosting', as they now like to say) was going to be demanding, but what was surprising was how <u>cheerful</u> it all was.

It does make me laugh to see how even the professional grumps in the press have been forced to join the national good mood. They must be <u>bursting</u> to tell some British-hopelessness story or a ghastly-foreigners story but they simply daren't be out of step with their readers.

One of the children's nannies used to tell them not to make faces because if the wind changed their faces would stay like that. Perhaps the wind will change now and those ill-tempered journalists will be stuck with a smile on their faces.

Maybe not.

Strangely, all this has made the last few days more tiring, not less. When I am simply being my normal self, everyone knows where they stand in the scheme of things. I am the Queen, they are the subjects. Conversation is polite and formal and stays safely on the surface of things.

But when people become relaxed, almost a bit <u>squiffy</u> with shared happiness, it is really altogether trickier. There's a danger that one can look a bit solemn or, worse (that greatest of modern crimes), 'out of touch'. So I have to be cheerful and relaxed, and yet dignified. It's surprisingly hard work.

Like many people, I had been secretly dreading the opening ceremony. One can have too much of what we now are supposed to call 'heritage'. I worried that it would be all Shakespeare and cream teas and bowler hats, or that the people organising it would try too hard to get away from the past with some ghastly line-up of girls or boys doing the dancing and singing acts that are now so popular.

Instead, it was like a rather odd dream. Those Victorians in funny hats. The nurses and doctors prancing around beds. We were all making fun of ourselves, but in an vaguely amusing way.

Then there was the helicopter business. As you know, I had my reservations about being part of a comic turn involving James Bond.

Although I've sat through several of the James Bond films, I have never been what you'd call a fan. Bond, with his smooth chat and caddish ways with women, reminds me of rather too many men I have met in my time. Andrew tried to be a Bond at one stage. Dear Tony Snowdon, when he was Antony Armstrong-Jones, managed it somewhat better, albeit in a slightly fey, pint-sized way. One of Catherine's cousins seems to be something of a rough-diamond, would-be Bond.

But Thrusting Justin in the press office was so keen. They said it would be 'ironic' (a word I have learned to distrust). Apparently, it would show the human face of modern monarchy. Then, when they told me the dogs would be part of the film, I began to think it could be really rather fun, at least for them. They do love a change to their routine.

I asked what would be involved. They told me that I

would have to walk along a corridor with Cider and Berry at my heels, and James Bond beside me. That didn't sound too difficult, I must say, and so I agreed.

How wrong can you be! We had agreed to let them do their filming in the rooms above the State Rooms. What the production team called their 'set-up' took most of the morning and, when I was told that they were ready to film me walking down the corridor, a scene of utter bedlam greeted me.

About 50 people were milling about, some with cameras or tape-recorders or tiny machines to show whether it was light enough. Young men were talking into mobile phones. Girls with clipboards strode about the place telling people what to do. They were all so busy that for a moment they didn't see me standing there with the dogs at my feet, watching them. When they did notice me, there was the usual fuss, ending up with people standing around in a semi-circle, gawking at me with the smiling, overawed expression I have come to know so well down the years.

A scruffy middle-aged man (the director, I assumed) introduced me to the actor playing James Bond, a chiselled, muscle-bound chap who did one of those showy bows that actors are so fond of.

I must say the filming took quite a lot longer than I expected. There was much fussing over James Bond's hair.

We did the scene with me sitting at a desk, ignoring James Bond while he waits, before doing our dialogue:

Me: Good evening, Mr Bond.

James Bond: Good evening, Your Majesty.

I managed that without too much difficulty. Then we

walked down the corridor and after that there was a huddle in the corner about how it all had gone.

The director thought that James Bond had not quite what he called 'nailed' the walk. It was more of a footman-walk rather than a Bond-walk (the walk is very important with Bond, apparently). He said Bond needed to look at me but not too much. 'Think helicopter,' someone said rather mysteriously.

Then, when he tried again, my old bitch Berry lost interest and wandered out of shot. Unwisely, one of the young men tried to pick her up and, well, you know she hates being pulled around by strangers, particularly men. Piercing screams, young man hopping about, holding his hand and using rather unnecessary language, embarrassment in the ranks, with much anguished muttering from James Bond about 'losing the moment', whatever that meant.

We 'took five', as the director put it. I calmed Berry, they calmed Bond. We tried again, this time with the dogs knowing that there was a treat in my handbag for them.

Eventually, the thing was done. The director simpered that 'Your Majesty is a born actress,' to which I replied with one of my cooler glances.

When I saw the film, I thought it was all perfectly harmless fun. If a committee of bright sparks has decided that the best way for our country to present itself to the world is as a nation that knows how to laugh at itself, then so be it. I was very happy to be part of the joke.

In the days following the opening ceremony, though, I did begin to wonder. The press office reported that they were receiving a large number of emails from children around the world who seemed to believe that I had indeed jumped out of a helicopter.

Not for the first time, it occurred to me that any kind of logic or basic common sense tends to go 'absent without leave' when anyone in this family does something even faintly unusual. People want to believe that we have the most extraordinary attributes, that we are like them and yet gifted in an almost divine way.

I suppose it was at that moment that I began to think it might be an idea, at this advanced age, for me to remind the world in some way or other that we are really not that different from them. A woman in her eighties does not jump out of a helicopter. She has worries and weaknesses, just like they do. It's a bit odd (and slightly unfair some-times) to believe otherwise.

Yours,

ER

Dear Sir Jeremy

What a sunny summary you have sent me! People are terribly good at being happy for a day or a weekend if there's some kind of special national occasion, but this has gone on for days, with not a sign of any 'backlash'.

Charles, who takes a great interest in these things, says it is all about what he calls 'self-image'. The world has been looking at us and, much to our surprise, it has liked what it sees. We feel liked, and therefore we become more likeable. It all sounds rather too good to be true, but then what do I know of such things?

I was slightly surprised that more was not made of Zara's silver medal in the three-day event. I seem to remember that there was quite a fuss when Anne was picked to ride for Britain many years ago. She was the first 'royal' to compete in the Olympics and so on.

Now her daughter (twice the horsewoman Anne ever was, but don't quote me!) has won a silver medal at the London games and no one turns a hair.

As you might expect, my dear husband the Consort has an explanation. He says that Zara has what he calls 'de-royaled' herself by talking in an accent that could be heard in any pub in London. She sounds like a waitress (I don't mean that in a snobbish way in the slightest), and so no longer attracts attention.

Accents matter. One's own has changed over the years, and so has Charles's. Anne, on the other hand, went out of her way to talk in a vaguely common way when she was in her twenties.

Zara has taken it a step further. Like her mother, she has not the slightest interest in being in the public eye. She would prefer to be out riding or at a party. When I talk to her, I'm aware that she is trying to talk in a way that is similar to mine, but is failing hopelessly. She has actually <u>forgotten</u> how to speak in her normal accent. I suppose she didn't want to be noticed and, instinctively, she sensed that the voice was where to start. She blended in.

Unfortunately, you can't be royal and speak with a typing-pool accent. It's expected that one talks in a certain way – rather oddly, when all the talk is of people becoming *less* conscious of class.

I'd say, to judge from the people I meet (including, above all, politicians and civil servants), that class counts as much today as it ever did, maybe more.

No doubt I'm hopelessly old-fashioned but it startles me to hear Zara speak. She is a sweet girl and commendably strong-minded, but I sense that something has been lost along the way. She seems further from us, as if, almost without knowing it, she has made a decision.

Am I imagining this, d'you think?

Yours,

ER

Dear Sir Jeremy

Thank you for your kind comments about the Consort. He was <u>furious</u> at having to stay in hospital. I do feel for those poor doctors.

I am getting on with life in the normal way, although I must say, it doesn't feel in the slightest bit normal. It's as if I have lost a limb. One does get so used to the presence of another person, always there, a couple of paces behind me, the laughter that's never far away when he's talking to people. I've never known anyone who could make people laugh so easily (when he wants to). I've always rather envied it.

The newspapers, as you will have seen, have decided, now that he's in hospital, that he's really rather marvellous after all – a bit rich, I must say, given the press he normally gets!

I can't bear to read any of those sick-making articles about our marriage. It seems to be something of a recent development, this poking around inside people's private lives. A marriage is a marriage. Trying to work out why it works, or doesn't work, is utterly futile.

Of course, now that he is not around, these things have been slightly on my mind. As you know, ours has never been a lovey-dovey marriage. I suspect most of the ones that last aren't. When Mr Blair (the Smiling Salesman, as you liked to call him) and his Cheshire-Cat wife stayed with us in Balmoral for a weekend, I noticed on several occasions when we were all in the sitting room that they were actually <u>holding hands</u>.

Am I being old-fashioned, Sir Jeremy, or is that not really rather peculiar? A grown-up married couple, with children and everything, holding on to each other in the presence of someone they don't even know very well.

Looking at them sitting there, like Tweedledum and Tweedledee, I wondered whether couples who go around hand-in-hand are clinging on out of fear rather than love, gripping the hand of husband or wife rather as a child clings to its nanny.

Company. Strength. Shared jokes. Loyalty. I've come to think that those are the big things in a marriage, not hand-holding and gazing into one another's eyes. I wouldn't <u>dream</u> of looking into the Consort's eyes. He would think I had gone quite mad. And the only time he looks me in the eye is when he's in a furious bate about something.

As with so much in life, one doesn't want to analyse these things too much, and certainly never in public. Things that are important between a husband and wife can fade when exposed to the light.

When I read that Mrs Blair actually told an interviewer that their last baby had been conceived at Balmoral, I'm afraid it confirmed my worst suspicions. I mean, honestly, does anyone want or need to know that kind of information? Surely, even in a time when showing off is accepted as perfectly normal behaviour, there are some things that should be kept private.

Sometimes when I read what the press says about the Consort, I can get quite annoyed. It's as if he is this cut-out figure who has never changed down the years. I wonder if they can have any idea of what it has been like for him.

He always knew he was going to make his mark in the world. That was what made me notice him. When I first met him, he was someone whom people instinctively looked up to, even older people. You could see it in the way he walked into a room, hear it in his voice. He was always going to be a leader.

Then, suddenly, all that had to change. He had to walk behind me, not because it was the polite thing to do but because I was the Queen. All eyes were on me. Of course, he had a more important role than ever but, in one sense, he was for ever going to be second-in-command – and to his wife.

He did what all great men can do. He adapted. He found a role for himself. He began to do things that the monarch could not (and would not!) do. He has opinions – I mean, he has opinions on everything, Sir Jeremy. He makes jokes. He asks the sort of awkward questions that other, less open people may think but keep to themselves.

Sometimes, it is quite uncanny how, when we are meeting people, he can read my mind. As some great person or local worthy explains something to me or says something more than usually fatuous, an opinion or question will form in my brain which I know is quite impossible for me to say out loud. Moments later I will hear my beloved Consort cheerfully blurt it out, no doubt ruffling a few official feathers and causing more silly newspaper stories.

A good thing, too. We need people like him. He hates pomposity (although I must confess that now and then he has been known to get on his high horse himself). Sometimes I think that the remarks he makes (the ones that seem to get him into trouble) are to remind the world, and himself, that, underneath it all, beyond the pomp and ceremony, none of us is as different from each other as we like to pretend.

I think that's rather a useful function, don't you? And, if he doesn't do it, who can? Charles tries now and then but humour's a tricky thing. It's like a horse that will only go for certain people. The Heir Apparent will sometimes give his humour a kick and advance on a joke, only to have the most crashing fall!

It is too easy to forget, as one gets older, the difficult times we have been through. While the children were growing, and I was still finding it quite tiring to balance the different parts of one's life, he could be quite impossible. Difficult, moody, really quite rude sometimes.

I'm not one who needs the arm around the shoulder and all that, but there were times when one really did feel rather alone. I suspect that he was a bit frustrated by the way his life had gone, and the only person he could take it out on was me.

There were rumours about girlfriends, of course. There are always rumours about girlfriends when a husband is good-looking and likes attractive, interesting people.

When some concerned busybody would, in cringing, apologetic tones, mention some item of gossip, I would be pretty cold towards him, I can tell you. I would thank him for keeping me up to date with the latest tittle-tattle and tell him that, if any more of the same came his way, I would be grateful if he kept it to himself.

That sort of business (even if the stories were true, which is highly doubtful in my view) becomes less important with time. Other less obvious things, friendship and conversation, are what last.

Things settled down. They just did. Things do tend to settle down in the end.

He has never been old, as far as I am concerned. I suspect that I have never been old to him. We have been together so long, and yet I still see that tall, confident young naval officer when I look at him. If someone mentions that he has been taken to hospital as a precautionary measure because of his age, my secret, instinctive reaction is one of surprise. Age? Philip? What on earth are they talking about?

It's the sort of thing that he can be terribly funny about, and he will be again very soon, I trust.

Yours,

ER

Dear Sir Jeremy

Thank you for guiding me, with your usual delicacy and tact, through this perilous terrain of the Paralympics and the words that should be used.

There was a time, really not so long ago, when no one thought twice about referring to someone as 'being crippled by arthritis' or 'left badly crippled after a hunting accident'. Suddenly that became a tricky word. Then 'handicapped' became a problem. It was, Thrusting Justin patiently explained to me, an old-fashioned term that implied some kind of inferiority. Between you and me, I couldn't quite see the difference between that and 'disabled', but I was glad of the advice. The last thing we need right now is a 'Queen in "handicapped" gaffe' headline. Only the Consort can get away with that.

Now you tell me that 'differently abled' is preferable to 'disabled', and I should be careful with 'deaf', 'dumb' or 'blind'. The seemingly innocent phrase 'wheelchair-bound' is on the banned list because a wheelchair should not be considered a restriction but a wonderful liberating thing.

How complicated it has all become.

I shall, of course, do as instructed, although I sometimes wonder where we are heading with all this. None of these words is actually inaccurate, but we now seem to prefer warm fogginess to truth. If I had just one leg, I would be rather insulted to be told that, compared to someone with two, I was not handicapped but differently abled.

It's as if words can make things better. If we say that being in a wheelchair is just as good as walking, then somehow it will be. Or am I missing something here?

William is terribly excited about the Paralympics. He says it's more 'real' (his favourite word) than the Olympics. When I asked him, during a telephone conversation last week, why a differently abled swimming contest is more real than a normal (can I say that?) one, the usual words one hears every day on the TV issued forth: 'moving', 'struggle', 'humbling'. It was the 'true face of sport'.

Of course, all that is true, and I'm glad that William is sensitive to these things in the modern way. But Sir Jeremy, is there not something slightly odd about what is going on out there? Most of the time, it is rather a struggle for those who suffer any kind of disability to get about or be noticed or taken seriously. Now, with London full of every kind of disability, people are cheering them on, and they are never off the TV. There is much dabbing of eyes and talk of how the achievements of these people 'put things into perspective'.

Of course, they do and it is moving, as any human struggle often is. But (perhaps it is my age) I have become rather suspicious of the emotion of crowds. When one is upset about something, it should surely be a private matter. These days it has become a group activity. You can see it in the kerfuffle that surrounds Children in Need Day, Comic Relief Day and Big Red Nose Day (or are they all the same thing?).

I even feel a little uneasy when I see people sobbing on Remembrance Sunday. Is this really the way those who have paid the ultimate sacrifice should be remembered? In some odd way, it puts the emphasis on the person feeling the emotion rather than the memory that caused it.

Of course, the Paralympics are going to be a wild success in modern Britain. All those stories of courage, all that overcoming the odds! How humble it makes us feel! It's like a marvellous combination of Big Red Nose Day and the Grand National.

Then, when the great army of the differently abled have left London, life will return to normal. Those who have to struggle to walk or who have something terribly wrong with them will be ignored by most people. The moment for tears and heroes will be over until we are all told that it's time to start feeling emotional again.

I'm afraid I might be old-fashioned about this. Margaret Rose was a terrible blubber when she was little. Our nanny used to say, 'And you can stop that showing off, Miss Margaret Rose.' I suppose Nanny Bristow would be thought heartless today but back then we knew exactly what she meant. Crying in front of other people was drawing attention to yourself, almost bullying them with your tears, trying to tell them that your emotion was what mattered.

It's why I secretly thought that the film *The King's Speech* was such utter bilge. We all knew that my father had a bit of a stutter and that it would be a problem when he became king. He was a straightforward man who knew his duty, so he took steps to have the problem fixed. That was that.

I find it slightly irritating that, as a result of this film, the memory of my father has now been infected with all

this <u>ridiculous</u> sentimentality about something that was
really never of great interest to him or anyone else.

The film makes him more 'human', I have been told.
Well, Daddy was certainly human but in rather more
important ways than the relatively trivial fact that he had a
stutter. Or should that be 'differently voiced'?

Yours,

ER

Dear Sir Jeremy

Thank you, as ever, for your latest Bulletin. I do enjoy reading what I call 'The Sir Jeremy News'! You have been my eyes and ears for longer than I care to remember, and I am eternally grateful to you.

It was kind of you to mention again how much you enjoy reading my letters in reply. To tell the truth, although I was terribly sad when you retired from the private office, these letters have been the most marvellous compensation for your company down the years. Being able to write to the world's most discreet man about the things that amuse or confuse or annoy me has truly been one of the more pleasurable activities of my old age.

It is, to use one of Charles's favourite phrases, 'excellent therapy', because there really is so much in modern life that is odd, intriguing or slightly shocking, isn't there? Reading the week's Sir Jeremy News, I sometimes find myself shaking my head in wonder at the madness of it all.

That is why I value our correspondence. I am involved in so many of these things, and have to be made aware of every twitch and rumble in the body politic, and yet, in a sense, I am also cut off from it all. When it comes to doing something, or even expressing an opinion, I am in a way less privileged than any of my subjects.

I sign papers. I agree to things. I ask tactful questions. I listen sympathetically as the prime minister of the moment explains how terrible everything is, and why it is all the fault of the last prime minister. But beyond making the right, polite noises, I am oddly powerless.

All this makes one think. There are questions in the mind, opinions. Sometimes, mulling over what has been going on, it is difficult to avoid getting quite cross.

Where can I do that? Where can I 'get it off my chest'? Not at work, of course, and not really at home. ('You haven't been thinking again, have you?' the Consort likes to say. 'I do wish you wouldn't.' He's only half-joking, maybe less than half.)

You know me well enough, Sir Jeremy, to be guessing by now that I am heading somewhere with this. I have a confession to make, which I fear is going to alarm you. Much as I appreciate your invaluable responses to my letters, I have been wondering recently whether we have not reached the stage when at least some of them might just possibly be of interest to a wider, more public audience than your good self.

I see you reaching for your pen, but hear me out. I am forever being told these days that we are in a new age of communication. As you know, some of the fizzier staff members in the press office have even suggested that William and Henry might 'keep in touch' by doing (is that the right word?) Facebook. At one meeting I attended, an equerry who shall remain nameless mentioned something called 'tweeting'. I thought he was joking until someone told me that a tweet can be a very serious thing. All very odd.

As you know, I am not at ease on the internet. When I hear the words 'click' and 'mouse' in the same sentence, my old brain shuts down until it all goes away. That's just the way I am.

And yet all around us there is this new, desperate need for communication. Suddenly, everyone wants to know what we're feeling or thinking. The ghastly Court correspondents make it all up by pretending they have spoken to a 'palace insider' or a 'source close to the Royal Family'. Then there are those endless films and plays in which an actress's version of me appears. I'm always this wise old bird, making beady comments with quiet humour.

How do they <u>know</u> what one is like? It becomes rather tiresome seeing oneself as a made-up character in the papers or on the screen, and never being able to say, 'Hold on, I'm not like that <u>in the very least</u>.'

I have reached a stage in my life when I would rather like people to see who I really am, read what I think and, just now and then, how I feel. My letters, if they were made public, would very discreetly be a part of this famous new age of communication. They will be respectful of whom I have met, whether it's the King of Jordan or Jordan, the top-heavy model (rather a favourite of mine, between you and me).

The views that I express will shock no one, being little more than those of any moderately observant woman in her eighties as she surveys the passing scene and thinks mildly about how it differs from other passing scenes of yesterday or the day before.

Would that be such a terrible idea, Sir Jeremy? A grandmother – and a great-grandmother – sharing her view of the world in an affectionate and curious way?

Please think hard about this before you reply. I value
your opinion above almost all others. Talking of which,
don't mention this idea to my dear husband. If he decides
to publish a book of thoughts and observations, I tremble
to think what might happen.

Yours,

ER

Dear Sir Jeremy

I do so enjoy the amusing final item in your Bulletins. It is always such a <u>relief</u> after what you call 'the hard news'. (Is it my imagination or is the news getting 'harder' as I get older?)

I'm always reminded of Sir Trevor McDonald and the twinkle that came into his eye when he said 'And finally . . .' Somehow it reassured us all that, whatever the madness that was in the headlines, the stuff of everyday life carries on.

This week I was intrigued by your remarks about happiness. As you so rightly point out, the days when people used to get on with things without worrying whether they were happy or not are well and truly gone. Today we all have to agonise over how we feel. Are we happier than we used to be? Are we happy enough? If we are happy now, is that a bad sign, which means that we'll be unhappy in the future? Is it the right <u>kind</u> of happiness? On and on it goes, and of course the more we worry, the more miserable we get.

And for some reason, it all has to be measured to make it real. Did I imagine it, or is there really now a department in government actually calculating the nation's Gross National Happiness? Frankly, nothing would surprise me.

I'm not the slightest bit surprised that universities now run Happiness Studies courses. No doubt there are long-faced professors of happiness gloomily studying these things in libraries all over the country.

It seems to me that the survey you tell me about is telling us what anyone with half a brain already knows. Work is important. You are more likely to find contentment doing a job that you enjoy than sitting in front of a TV or gazing vacantly into the void (sometimes pretty much the same thing).

Between you and me, I have worried a lot about work and the children down the years. I am fortunate enough to have had a job that, with all its occasional tiresomeness, brings it own rewards. I visit, I meet people, I express mild interest in what they are doing, I move on and, sometimes mysteriously to me, I make their day. There is in all this what they call 'job satisfaction'.

Things have been trickier for the four children. Charles, after several false starts, has found a role for himself. He has the Prince's Trust, spreading good works, and there is his private 'Kitchen Cabinet' where his favourite intellectuals (Stephen Fry, Jonathon Porritt, Alan Titchmarsh) consider the great issues of the day. He has become the unofficial royal conscience.

Anne is fine, too. Being a confident person, she has managed to divide her life rather neatly. She does her round of duties in a brisk, slightly impatient way, and then gets on with what really matters to her – horses, dogs, gymkhanas and so on.

It is the other two who have been the real worry. I look at Andrew now, a burly chap in a blazer, forever at work on some hopeless new business enterprise, and wonder whether we could have helped him more. He thinks of himself as a businessman, an ambassador for what he rather shy-makingly calls 'UK Plc'. At every possible opportunity he gets on an aeroplane to meet entrepreneurs on the other side of the world.

He dreams of being Richard Branson, but in reality he's nearer to Mark Thatcher. I have an awful feeling that some of the men in suits don't take him entirely seriously. When he introduces me to some shifty-eyed entrepreneur from Azerbaijan, I notice that there is a certain lack of attention from the other man as my son starts talking about mission statements, road maps, the bottom line and so on. I know absolutely nothing about business but sometimes it seems to me, listening as Andrew rattles on about his latest scheme, that there is rather more in it for the Azerbaijanian chap than for UK Plc.

When I mentioned that to Andrew, he became slightly flustered and told me that I didn't understand business. It was essential that I sing from the same hymn-sheet while he got his ducks in a row, he said.

The truth is that if he had not been born into the family, he would have been quite content as a middle-order business chap, diarising meetings, flirting with secretaries and playing the occasional round of golf with the chairman. Somehow, being royal and being at what he likes to call 'the sharp end' just don't quite go together.

I mentioned once to Charles that perhaps his younger brother might be given a role within the Duchy of Cornwall (sales manager for the shortbread division, perhaps) but received a very dusty answer. It seems that even Charles, who shudders at the sight of a brown envelope and wouldn't know a balance sheet if it bit him on the nose, has a distinctly low opinion of Andrew's entrepreneurial skills.

Then there is Edward. Oh dear. Of all the children, 'Teddy Edward', as he was known when he was a boy, was the most thoughtful and kind. By the time he arrived on the scene, the Consort had rather gone off the boil so far as taking an interest in the children was concerned, and so Teddy Edward was allowed to be himself.

From quite an early stage, he tended to the artistic side of things. By the time he was 10, he had lost interest in riding or shooting, and had taken to sitting in his room, reading his books, and playing his computer games. Sometimes, he told me, rather to my alarm, he just liked to think about things.

He first mentioned an interest in 'the media' when he was about 13. It was quite a shock. The Queen Mother, who was always fond of Edward, asked what exactly he meant by 'the media'? 'Some sort of communication,' he said.

I imagine we all had the identical thought at that point. If there was one thing at which Teddy Edward did not excel, it was communicating. When his father asked him how he was getting on at school, or why he always had his head in a book rather than getting some exercise like other boys of his age, there was much stammering and 'y'knows' and 'not really sures', at the end of which none of us was any the wiser.

It was when Edward murmured something about reading Media Studies at university that we all became seriously alarmed. There is a limit. After he managed a couple of modest A-levels, we sent him off to New Zealand in the hope that a tough, old-fashioned place like that would sort him out. After that there was Cambridge, which seemed to have done Charles no lasting harm.

In retrospect, the decision to knock the 'media studies' business out of him with a spell in the marines was a bad idea. It was a difficult time. There were rather too many calls week by week, his voice at the other end seeming smaller and more plaintive with every one. We had guessed that he was not cut out to be one of life's marines well before his commanding officer rang to tell us, somewhat apologetically, that he thought Edward was not quite 'army material'.

To be fair to him, the Consort took it rather better than one might have anticipated. A certain chill descended upon relations, and occasional sarcastic remarks were made, but it was generally accepted in the family that there was no escaping the fact that Edward was 'artistic'.

Let's not talk about his first idea, *It's a Royal Knockout*. I suppose it's what happens when you give a creative young chap his head. Nothing really matters on TV, but I must say that watching members of the Royal Family scampering about an arena in fancy dress with Cliff Richard, Barbara Windsor and the Blackadder man, with Teddy Edward trying to do jokes and poor Anne looking like thunder, is a memory that haunts me to this day. So <u>this</u> was where Edward's 'communication' led – to Sarah Ferguson doing the three-legged race with Les Dawson!

After that debacle, we became used to Edward looming on family occasions with a cine-camera in front of his face. 'Smile, Mummy,' he would say, adding sometimes, 'Now, loves, just say something completely natural, pretend I'm not here.'

It was perfectly harmless, once we had established with him that none of his shaky home movies would ever, under any circumstance, be seen outside the family. I believe they are in a box in one of the palace store-rooms.

The dream of being creative lived on. When he came to see us, he would insist on telling us about a marvellous new novel by someone we had never heard of. Every Christmas I received a hardback book or some poems from him, in spite of my gently telling him that I have quite enough to read with all my boxes and correspondence and I get rather more poetry than I need in letters from schoolchildren.

Did work made Teddy Edward happy? I suppose for a while it did. Like many artistically inclined young men of his generation, he set up a production company. He was terribly lit up about it for a few years, forever telling us about the latest dotty-sounding project that was 'in development'. His conversation became distressingly full of 'loves', 'darlings' and even, when he was in full flow, 'loveys'.

Poor Edward. As with his few weeks in the marines, it all ended in tears. I suspect that, like Andrew, he found that his royal connection was more of a hindrance than a help when it came to getting on in civilian life. His company went quietly bust, and after that there was less talk of films he was going to make.

Sophie settled him down, and these days he potters about, opening this or that, a useful person to field for events that the rest of us are too busy to attend.

No doubt he misses those days when he was 'something

in the media', and still believed, sweet boy, that he was going to be a great director. I'll always remember the smile on his face when, in the middle of a family occasion, he would 'frame' a scene with his hands, making a square in front of his face, and murmur something about what a marvellous light it was.

Yours,

ER

Dear Sir Jeremy

I was so sorry to hear that your cat Proust has been causing you worry. 16 years is a good age but I'm sure there is more life in the old boy yet. I certainly hope so.

It is funny how, after a while, our animals almost become part of our characters. I often imagine you in your flat in Pimlico, with Proust beside you on the sofa. This joint-being, Sir Jeremy/Proust, half-private secretary/half-cat, looks at the world through narrowed eyes. He has seen it all, and knows more than he will ever tell. Now and then, sometimes when you least expect it, Sir Jeremy/Proust will take a swipe at the world, just to show that he shouldn't be taken for granted.

People who have not loved a dog or a cat can never quite understand the position our animals take up in our lives. When everything is complicated, they can be relied upon. While humans flail about, trying to understand this or that, they just <u>know</u>.

It is more than comfort, or company, or any of those little things. They are part of your life, sometimes reading your thoughts before you have had them, every day reminding you that, whatever crisis is unfolding, we all need a walk, or food, or (not literally, of course) a reassuring scratch behind the ear.

The awful thing is that, when one of the dogs or one of the horses has to be put down, I find it more upsetting than the loss of a person. I'm not saying that animals are better or more important than people (although sometimes it's difficult to avoid that conclusion), simply that they reach a different part of the human heart.

When the moment comes to call the vet, the loss feels so very personal. For all those years, they have trusted you to feed them, exercise them and keep them warm, and in return they have given you fierce (in the case of Sherry rather <u>too</u> fierce) loyalty. And now you are calling someone over to kill them.

I'm sure that you have these feelings as powerfully with your cat Proust as I have with any of the dogs, but as I think you know, I suffer from an unchanging lifelong prejudice. I've always thought dogs were altogether better, more admirable citizens of the world than cats.

It's not just the cruelty of cats (think of the millions of luckless birds that are killed by them every day), but their general slyness, the sneaky way they slip in and out of doors, their general lack of what the Consort calls 'moral fibre'.

Look at your Proust lying there, Sir Jeremy. Can you in all honesty say that you could depend on his loyalty? You can tell a cat's character in the way it looks at you. The way they narrow their eyes – it's like a human putting on a fake smile. There's absolutely <u>nothing</u> sincere about a cat. They might occasionally be brighter than some dogs (a Lurcher, say, or a rather dense King Charles Spaniel), but their cunning is <u>always</u> self-centred. They're like foxes in that way.

Of course, some people find the directness and honesty of a dog a bit off-putting. They prefer a lurking, unreliable, miaouing creature, seeing perhaps something of their own personality there.

Writers and artists have cats. Most modern politicians prefer them. Dogs are owned by people in business, those who need to be in charge, certainly actors. They require an element of straight dealing, a bit of honest authority from their person, and some people (cat people) find this difficult. It makes them feel bossy. They prefer to wheedle and coo in the manner expected by cats.

Humans can be divided into dogs or cats, too. The Head Boy is a dog, the Smiling Salesman was a cat. Mr Osborne and Mr Balls are dogs, of course. The ghastly Heseltine man was a cat, as was that purring nonentity, John Major. Neil Kinnock, oddly, was very much of a dog (albeit of the yappy variety).

Then there are those confusing cases of people who really should be one thing but try to pretend they're the other. That rather creepy Mr Mandelson is a cat through and through but, with typical cattish deviousness, owns a dog to throw us all off the track. You, on the other hand, are one of life's dogs in spite of the fact that your closest friend in the world is a cat called Proust (why Proust by the way? Isn't it a type of biscuit?). Please don't be insulted by my calling you a dog, Sir Jeremy. It's the highest compliment. And don't mention this letter to Proust. You know how huffy cats can get if they feel they are not being taken as seriously as they expect to be.

Yours,

ER

Dear Sir Jeremy

I had not realised that Catherine's sister Philippa had written a book, and am most grateful to you for drawing it to my attention.

If the newspaper extracts are anything to go by, it is a perfectly straightforward guide to entertaining, although I am always slightly surprised by what people need to be advised about these days.

The disagreeable remarks in the press surprise me less than they do you. Whenever there is an unusual amount of unpleasantness being written about someone these days, it can almost always be explained in one word: jealousy.

This poor Philippa girl (we've only met briefly) was bound to get it in the neck from the press after the very odd (and uninvited) publicity she received at William and Catherine's wedding.

I suppose I'm terribly out of touch these days, but I did find it quite extraordinary that in 2013 a girl can be treated like that. She wore a perfectly smart and respectable dress and yet suddenly, for no obvious reason, the press became fixated, in really the most ridiculous and vulgar way, on her figure.

Once it was only the grubby papers at the popular end of the market who behaved like this. Now both the press and television seem to have become infected. Entire pages in apparently serious newspapers have been devoted to one part of the luckless girl's anatomy.

What on earth is going on, Sir Jeremy? Not so long ago, what a person found attractive was a private matter. Possibly one chap might say to another, in a mess, canteen or office somewhere, 'I say, that Pippa girl has a jolly nice figure, hasn't she?' (or words to that effect) but nothing more than that.

Since when has physical attraction become a national sport? Were those ridiculous Page 3 models in the tabloid newspapers to blame? I never thought they were a good idea and long ago asked Mrs Thatcher whether something could be done. It was almost the only time during our audiences when she was lost for words.

I can't believe it's healthy, this sudden shared fascination with some bewildered girl. The Consort, reading this Philippa nonsense at breakfast, described it as 'boggling'. In the past few decades we do seem to have become a nation of bogglers.

Looking back, it was perhaps that photograph of Diana, taken soon after she became engaged to Charles, that started the rot. You'll remember the one: she was looking after some children and a photograph was taken with the sun behind her so that one could see the shape of her legs.

At first, I was embarrassed on behalf of her and the photographer. What a ghastly mistake, I thought. Then, as the picture appeared again and again, it dawned on me that it hadn't been a mistake at all. Poor Diana, who had yet to learn the tricks of the trade at that point, had been duped.

There was a certain amount of tut-tutting, but soon it was clear that across the nation everyone was having a good old gawp at a young girl's legs. And not even furtively, in the old-fashioned way, but quite openly.

That was when it all started. It became acceptable for people to look at a member of the royal family as an object of fantasy. This boggling was almost part of their loyalty and love. <u>Most</u> unattractive.

Of course, the person who is at the centre of it all is utterly helpless. If she tries to look modest or avoid the public gaze, that strangely seems to inflame them all the more.

Eventually, liked scorned lovers everywhere, they turn on her. They blame the person who has done this to them by looking the way she does. They seek ways in which they can punish her, or at least pay her back for not being what they expected (not that they know what that is).

I'm sure Philippa will know how to handle all this (girls today are so much better at that sort of thing than we were), but I do feel sorry for her.

Yours,

ER

Dear Sir Jeremy

Thank you for keeping me up to date with ever-more depressing news about the ghastly new railway that is being planned. How glad I am that it will not be me who has to take the inaugural trip on it.

When I see what it will do to the Chilterns, the parts of Warwickshire where I hunted when I was a child, the lovely houses it will blight, the farmland cut in half, the fields and hedges and woods destroyed, I do wonder whether it is worth all that money, not to mention all the political rows that will rumble on for years.

As it happens, the Head Boy gave me a 'briefing' this week (although brief it was not) on the new trains. He must be doing better in the polls at the moment because he was insufferably bumptious and pleased with himself. This super new railway will save businessmen a whole 20 minutes off a journey from London to Birmingham, he told me.

'Goodness,' I said quietly. 'A whole 20 minutes?'

Mr Cameron's no fool, and my tone of light mockery was not lost on him. He crossed his legs, a sure sign that he's about to enter full Head Boy mode, and delivered a lecture. Our conversation (including what I would have liked to say, but couldn't) went something like this:

Head Boy: Your Majesty, the great thing about HSR2 – and this really is absolutely crucial – is that it will drive growth in a very sustainable way. It's an absolutely vital investment in our country's long-term future, delivering positive outcomes for jobs and ending the north-south divide (and so on for another five minutes).

Me: Of course. (It always comes down to growth. Saving a man in a suit 20 minutes in his busy day is more important than anything else. I've seen it before, I'm afraid. What the Treasury wants, the Treasury gets.)

Head Boy: And of course we shall be very conscious of the need to mitigate environmental impact with tunnels, cuttings, and we shall be very sensitive to (continue for another five minutes).

Me: Yes. (And the unfortunate people who are in the way of the train will doubtless be called 'nimbies'. What a *very* unattractive expression that is. If the people who live in a beautiful part of England are not prepared to speak up for it, then who is? If Windsor Great Park or the estate at Sandringham or Balmoral were under threat, I would be among the nimbies.)

Head Boy: It's tremendously important internationally, Your Majesty. It will show the world for once and for all that Britain is open for business.

Me: Yes, that's very important. (Perhaps it is a sign of age, but I think more and more that each of us has a duty to the part of the country that we know and love. Those backyards are our personal kingdoms, and need protecting above all else.)

Head Boy: The view from Whitehall is very much that a balance must be maintained between the needs of growth and of heritage (and off he went for another five minutes).

Oh dear. I tuned out at that stage and let him burble on

until he told me he had another important meeting to attend.

Almost every word of what he said made me feel so tired that, as soon as I reached Sandringham yesterday, I took the dogs for a walk to the walled kitchen garden, one of my favourite refuges here at Sandringham, to think it all through.

Apart from the raspberries, potatoes and our wonderful Jerusalem artichokes, most of the beds are being prepared for winter. None of the gardeners were there, and so I sat on a bench near the old fig tree and pondered your letter. Where better to think about growth than in a kitchen garden?

Perhaps the truth is that my life is so different from the lives of those people scurrying about in the city that sometimes I forget that many of them see things differently from people like me. It's not that they can't see the wood for the trees, but that they can't see the wood at all. It's simply a product, used to provide them with a desk or a dining-room table. Where it comes from concerns them no more than the origin of a bit of plastic or metal.

Mr Cameron's 'view from Whitehall' is one filled with houses, streets, buildings, cars and fumes. The only things that are meant to grow there are salaries, jobs and the economy.

There is another view, held by those of us who live in the country, but because we are governed by city-dwellers, the way the rural minority see things has begun to seem peculiar and eccentric. If we love the landscape and want to protect it from slow destruction, we are considered to be 'nimbies'.

The great, unspoken division in our society, far stronger than class, or perhaps even race, is that between the majority who live in towns and those who live in the country. If Garnham, the gardener, who has been at Sandringham for simply years, had wandered into the kitchen garden as I sat thinking about all this with the dogs, I should have felt as if I had more in common with him than with the Archbishop of Canterbury (not difficult, I grant you), or virtually any government minister, or even you.

I always notice that when we have rather grand visitors down from London for the weekend (Hillary Clinton, say, or those tiresome Sarkozys), how out of place they look with their smart weekend outfits (the green is always slightly too bright on country clothes sold in the town), their soft skins, the way they sit close to the fire as if the place is cold. We go for walks and I realise that, although they look about them and make polite conversation, they are seeing nothing. They might as well be looking at it all on a cinema screen.

I feel sorry for them – and for you, Sir Jeremy! I'm aware that your heart is in Pimlico. You used to dread that moment when, during one of your very occasional forays out of London, I would produce a spare pair of gumboots so that you could come for a walk. You were distinctly wobbly when, years ago, one of the Lurchers caught a rabbit and I had to finish it off.

It takes a long time for someone used to the town way of doing things to become a country person – sometimes they never do. You just have to hear the way people talk about animals (those dangerous foxes in suburban gardens!) or changes in the weather, to know that most of us have become so soft and citified that nature is seen as something dangerous and threatening.

I thought about this a lot when Michael and Carole Middleton visited us during that rather tense period after William and Catherine had become engaged.

Have you met the Middletons? They're a sweet couple, as kind and sensible as anyone could hope. There's much to be said for additions to the family who have had to make their own way in the world. The grander families who have come into the fold, as it were, have a tendency to think they know more than they do. They are too confident for their own good. There's no fool like a titled fool.

It was the most terrific success, the Balmoral visit of Michael and Carole, if a little strained to start with with them sitting up straight in their armchairs as if they were being interviewed for a job – but they were soon quite at ease and terribly interesting about the work they do. I had absolutely no idea that 'partyware' was such a cut-throat business!

But, good people as they are, neither of them was entirely at ease in the country. They are the type of family who will have a 'carport' and electric gates and a lawn that is mown to within an inch of its life.

The Consort suggested, really by way of making conversation, that Michael might like to do a bit of stalking and, rather to our surprise, they were both enthusiastic about the idea. They were part of a shooting syndicate down in Hampshire but had never shot a stag.

Ever-willing, we arranged a day out with Angus, our

most reliable ghillie. Although he's ancient these days, Angus is terribly good with VIPs – he was a *great* favourite of Ronald Reagan's, who used to send him a Christmas card every year.

Angus told me that there was an old stag who had reached the end of his days and was suitable for beginners, being too doddery on his old pins to go far, so off went the Middletons in the Land Rover at the crack of dawn.

It was not an unqualified success. They returned at tea-time, muddy and ashen-faced. The stag had been found, having been gently stalked as it made its creaky way over hill and glen. Unfortunately, by the time it was in range, they had 'bonded' with it and enthusiasm for the outing had definitely waned. It was decided in a muttered conversation between them that, if the news was leaked that Catherine's father (or worse, mother) had slaughtered an innocent stag, it could be bad PR. I suspect that Angus was thoroughly relieved – it's a lot easier to cull old stags without distinguished guests agonising over the process – and the Middletons clearly heaved a sigh of relief.

The important thing, they both agreed over tea, was to have seen a 'magnificent' stag. Carole admitted, having watched the stag all day, she had become rather fond of it, and was glad it had been 'spared'.

I'm sure that one day they will feel at home in the real countryside but seeing them there, with their neat clothes splattered in mud, I realised how strange it all was to them.

It will take a while for them to understand the country, just as it does for a politician to understand why destroying fields and hedges for a ridiculous new train line is a bad idea.

Yours,

ER

Dear Sir Jeremy

Few surprises in the coverage of Catherine and William's announcement, I'd say. The overexcited headlines, the slightly impertinent speculation, the gushing reports of 'court correspondents', the nudging puns. At least, since the poor girl's in hospital, we are spared the overuse of the word 'radiant'. From what William has said, she is feeling anything but radiant right now.

Sometimes I think I'm getting a little old for all this, Sir Jeremy. It's as if no one has been in the family way before. Like so much else, the business of having a baby has become the excuse for yet another great emotional outpouring.

When I had Charles, back in the mists of time, there was of course a certain amount of excitement in the papers, but there was also respect. A couple bringing a new person into the world was seen as a private thing, even if that person happened to be a future king.

Now everyone has to be in on the act, and often in rather a tasteless way. Every stage of Catherine's pregnancy will be snapped and analysed. People really do seem to behave as if, by some curious process, she is part of their family. The press will start fussing as soon as she does anything more energetic than walking rather slowly. Is she eating enough? Or too much? Is she happy? Or sad? Is William seeing enough of her?

She will be described as a 'mum-to-be' and 'blooming'.

Can you imagine me being described as a blooming mum-to-be 60 years ago?

Then those long-lens lizards of the press will start taking photographs. I do find this fascination with the figures of famous women who are pregnant rather odd. There will soon be those frightful references to 'the bump'.

The daughter of one of my ladies-in-waiting is pregnant and has noticed that people now seem to feel the need to lay their hands on her 'bump'. It's all very odd. Even people she has only just met, including men, cheerfully and without permission reach forward and feel her stomach. These days when we're so sensitive about what Charles calls 'invasion of personal space', it's surprising that nobody worries about this.

I suppose that having a baby has become something of a public act, the one part of family life in which everyone has a right to share.

William, I suspect, will become a rather marginal figure in the coming months. The focus of the world will be on Catherine and then, increasingly, her bump.

It is all very indelicate and, between you and me, I thoroughly disapprove.

Yours,

ER

Dear Sir Jeremy

It was inevitable, I suppose, that there should be speculation in the press about the name that William and Catherine will choose for their baby. Apparently, Diana and Elizabeth are the bookies' favourites. (Have you noticed that everything – but everything – can now be subject of a bet? It's as if something isn't quite real until Ladbrokes or William Hill have quoted a price for it.)

Inevitably, the infant will be given a press name to reflect the way he or she is seen by the public. Diana became 'Di', which made her sound like a writer for a women's magazine, but also made her more approachable. Sarah was far too quiet for the wife of Andrew, so she had to be 'Fergie'.

For their own unfathomable reasons, the press decided that Andrew was a bit of a bounder – 'Andy' fitted the bill perfectly. The other children, Charles and Anne, have been spared the process. 'Eddie' never quite worked for dear, sweet Edward, in spite of the efforts of the press to make him rather more raffish than, in fact, he is.

It was Diana who first noticed the way this happened. When Henry, while at prep school, announced that no one was called Henry these days and that he would much prefer to be 'Harry', the Consort and I were not keen. We both thought that Harry made him sound like a bookmaker on the rails at Plumpton.

How wrong we were. Henry has made the name 'Harry' his own. It allows him to be the character, the wild card that the media require at all times from my family. (Andy has become Andrew, you will notice, now that he no longer plays that role.) Some of the stories attributed to 'Harry', the parties and so on, would seem downright odd if he were Henry.

William, on the other hand, will be allowed to keep his name. He is not a Will or a Bill or Billy or a Willie, thank goodness. The half-hearted press nickname 'Wills' was never going to last.

It is a great, underrated achievement to have managed to remain his own, sweet, straightforward self.

Yours,

ER

Dear Sir Jeremy

It was thoroughly wicked of you to send me such a detailed report of my visit to 10 Downing Street for a Cabinet meeting. It is <u>not</u> something I particularly wanted to be reminded of.

To tell the truth, Sir Jeremy, I am often rather surprised by today's politicians. All the bowing and scraping that goes on! I'm sure that, until 20 or 50 years ago, there was a general feeling that we were on the same side. Mr Macmillan was relaxed to a fault. Mr Wilson and Mr Heath were reasonably at ease with one. Now, though, there is tremendous sucking up and cow-eyes all round. It is as if they've become members of the public.

The more I see of the way we are governed, the more worried I become about the future, and this distinctly odd event did nothing to change my mind. Endless photographs were taken of the 'historic' occasion (everything is 'historic' these days). I was introduced to the Cabinet, one or two of whom I knew, and a few I recognised from the TV.

The meeting itself was every bit as dull as I had feared it would be. The Head Boy announced the importance of it all in the cheeky-but-respectful manner he seems to think is charming. There was some rather tiresome bantering. Mr Clarke, the one who seems to have been around for years and always needs a haircut, was rather too full of himself for my liking.

The Head Boy explained (by way of a joke, I imagine) that this was a Coalition cabinet and that I would see how well his party worked with their Liberal Democrat colleagues. When I asked if the Liberal Democrats sat together during Cabinet meetings, there was much fake jollity.

'Good Lord, we have to keep them apart, Ma'am,' said Mr Clarke.

There was then more joshing around the table, with poor bewildered Mr Clegg trying to show his humorous side (that was never going to work).

'No, no, we're just one big happy family, Ma'am,' he kept saying.

'Yes,' bellowed the appalling Mr Clarke. 'We all hate each other.'

Rather taken aback by this outbreak of hilarity, I tried to move things on. 'How frightfully amusing you all are,' I said coldly.

This is what the Consort calls a 'crinkler', and it usually works a treat. On this occasion, though, the crinkler went soaring over their heads, and was treated like yet another most tremendous joke. I kept rather quiet after that.

Once the meeting started, they were all on their best behaviour, leaning forward to listen or now and then to give an earnest little report on this or that.

There were no disagreements, and any jokes were of the political kind (unfunny, in other words). It really was like being a VIP visiting one of our better public schools and being invited to attend a school council where favoured sixth formers and teachers meet.

The mention of happy families sent me into a not unpleasant little daydream about my childhood when we used to play games with Miss Crawford in the nursery.

Do they still have that game Happy Families, Sir Jeremy? Mrs Mug the Milkman's wife and so on? To pass the time, I found myself giving names to members of the Cabinet. The round personage with the creepy soft handshake, Mr Pickles, was an obvious choice for Mr Bun the Baker, and I thought that the overkeen Gove chap could be Mr Test the Teacher. Obviously, Mr Osborne was Mr Chop the Butcher. I was trying to find a character for the demented-looking Justice Minister (sorry, the name escapes me) when the Head Boy drew the meeting to a close.

Never have I been more relieved to be back with the dogs at BP.

Yours,

ER

Dear Sir Jeremy

I do believe you're accusing me of 'sexism'! Of course some
women were present at the Cabinet meeting. I definitely
remember the Home Secretary (or Mrs Trim the Tailor's
Wife as I came to think of her). I'm almost sure there were
others but their faces do tend to merge into one middle-
aged woman – bright, bossy, but oddly unimpressive, who
only pops up when sent off to face Jeremy Paxman on
Newsnight after something has gone wrong and the men
have decided to keep their heads down!

There are moments when I wonder whether politics are
terribly good for women. Somehow we are too sensible not
to be sent round the bend eventually by the silly games
involved. That nice Shirley Williams, who was once relatively sane, now can hardly draw breath she talks so much.
I used to be able to have a tremendous gossip with Harriet
Harman (her ambition as a girl was to be a ballet dancer,
you know) but now she has become *very* frowny and
disapproves of virtually everything, me in particular.

Then there was Mo Mowlam, who became rather too
full of herself towards the end, and that Mrs Smith, another
Home Secretary (is there something in the job title that
makes the men think it suitable for a woman, d'you
think?), who had to stand down when her husband was
caught watching rude films (how the Consort laughed!).
And Mrs Thatcher, who had to win at everything, and had
no discernible sense of humour whatsoever.

I'm not saying that they were bad at their jobs (most of them were more effective than men), just that being looked at, listened to, praised, sucked up to and insulted around the clock has a more noticeable long-term effect on women than it does on men.

Sooner or later, they begin to crack – rather like Angela Rippon suddenly appearing on the *Morecambe and Wise Show* and doing the can-can dance. Fame simply became too much for her.

I've always found men far easier to deal with. They're less complicated. Even when they're untrustworthy (which is most of the time), they're untrustworthy in a predictable way. You can depend on them, rather as you can with dogs. They may be absolute devils and deserve to be given a good sorting-out now and then, but at least one knows where one stands with them.

Women are cats, Sir Jeremy, and, as you know, that is not always a compliment in my book.

Yours,

ER

Dear Sir Jeremy

Oh dear, I see that our quiet pre-Christmas family gathering has attracted the attention of the press. How depressing it is that dear Prince Michael and his long-suffering wife Marie Christine should once more be in the firing line of 'royal correspondents'. For rather too long, she has been a lightning rod for negative stories in the press, with all those ridiculous and unfair slurs – 'Princess Pushy' and so on.

It seems that the newspapers have to have a villain in this family, someone on whom to vent all the jealousy and resentment that can't be expressed against its principle members, and poor Marie Christine fits the bill perfectly. She's foreign, independent-minded and, most important of all, a woman.

As you know, Sir Jeremy, I am not exactly what you would call a women's libber, but I do find it strange that the very people who would normally make a fuss about sexism are quite <u>loathsome</u> on TV about the way certain women look, talk or behave if they happen to disapprove of them. Anne was horribly mocked at one point, then poor old Sarah. Now it's Marie Christine.

I have often joked with her (she has a terrific sense of humour) that the rest of us owe her a debt of gratitude for taking all the nasty comments that 'court correspondents' can dream up. Every time she makes any kind of remark, there is a fuss. She said she was one of the tallest people to marry into the family (true), that she was brighter than most of us (undeniable), and that more royal blood flowed through her veins than through the veins of any other member of the family, with the exception of the Consort (and what of it?).

I simply can't understand what they have against Marie Christine. She costs the taxpayer nothing. She earns a respectable living, writing books, doing interior decoration and running art galleries. She represents us and does charitable work. She's attractive and often amusing. Does all that make a woman 'pushy' in 2013?

If now and then she goes a little far (the gold-plated calling cards were rather a mistake, I always thought, and the appearance on *Royals and Their Pets* was definitely misjudged), is it really so serious?

Personally, I think we need more strong women like her. Don't you?

Yours,

ER

Dear Sir Jeremy

Thank you for drawing my attention to events in Holland in the latest bundle you have sent me. I have always been rather fond of Queen Beatrix, and was not a bit surprised to read in your very helpful briefing document that she has what you call 'high approval ratings' among her people. She has high approval ratings with me, too.

I never knew that people over there called her 'Bea'. It seems an odd way to address your sovereign, Queen Bea, but then they are Dutch and I suppose one should make allowances.

It was good of you to remind me that a handwritten note was in order – I've never known a private secretary with such a perfect sense of correct procedure! I shall write to her today.

Does one congratulate or commiserate on an abdication, do you think?

Out here in the country, watching the garden and the fields slowly come to life after the awful cold and floods, I have been giving much thought to Beatrix's speech. She looked like a women at peace with the world, didn't she? She said something about her 'beautiful task' having given her much satisfaction and, you know, I think she meant it. At that moment, Sir Jeremy, I experienced a feeling that was almost like envy.

Our task has never been exactly beautiful, has it? Whether it's one member of the family being photographed

without her clothes on by some ghastly photographer
lurking in the undergrowth, or another being criticised for
saying that as a soldier in a war he shot at people (what
else, pray, is a soldier meant to do?), all in all, beauty has
been rather hard to come by.

It set me thinking, what Beatrix said. Perhaps the reason
why she looks so happy is that she hasn't had to linger. She
knew she was going to stand down. Is there a lesson here
for us, I wonder?

I know that the Dutch Royal Family has a history of
retiring, but surely there's a case for the old getting out
of the way of the young – or, in our case, of the slightly
less old.

I am just thinking out loud here, Sir Jeremy, but I would
welcome your thoughts.

Yours,

ER

Dear Sir Jeremy

Thank you for your detailed memo. It was most kind of you to remind me of the constitutional position, and of the high affection in which I am held by the British people, not to mention the crisis of national confidence that would be caused by the possibility of 'a virtually unprecedented change of circumstance at the top'.

I am fully aware that the Dutch are different from us. I have had a running commentary on that very topic from the Consort. At breakfast this morning, a voice from behind the *Daily Telegraph* informed me that they take drugs, the Dutch, quite openly in restaurants in Amsterdam. It's legal, he said. 'Steak and chips, bottle of plonk and a big fat reefer, please, waiter.'

I said I was not sure it was quite like that, but then he was off again.

'And they're world leaders when it comes to bumping people off,' he said. 'There's a bill going through the Dutch parliament that will allow anyone over 70 to go to their GP and say, "Morning, doctor, I've completed my life. Now please kill me." ' He said it would never work here. 'There'd just be another bloody NHS queue,' was the way he put it.

But I do wonder why you are so concerned that I should be thinking, in a vague and private way, about some form of retirement. Why are the old in this country suddenly so afraid of letting go of their position in the world? Bruce Forsyth doing his desperate little tap-dance on the dancing programme. Women newsreaders complaining that they've been stood down from their duties too early. Those ridiculous Rolling Stones scampering about on their doddery old pins, singing about love and girls when everyone knows that all they really want is a nice cup of tea and an early bed.

Quite often when one of these overactive pensioners appears at the palace, and totters up to get a knighthood, I'm tempted to say, 'Well done, Mick (or Elton or Paul or whoever it is). Now go home, put your slippers on and let other people have a go. Your time is up.'

Apparently, one's not supposed to say this sort of thing any more. The last time I saw the Head Boy at one of our weekly meetings, he bounced in, all shiny-faced and dimply, and started talking about a new pensions bill. When I asked why people had to go on working into old age when there was meant to be a shortage of jobs, he gave me a little lecture about how there's now a pension time-bomb.

Another time-bomb! A bit like last year's obesity time-bomb but this time it's not the fat who are going to explode but the old.

We just can't afford for people to stop working, the Prime Minister said. Besides, people want to work on. They see it as their right.

But why? I keep thinking of the words we used to hear in church: 'To every thing there is a season, and a time to every purpose under heaven.' Surely that includes the old getting out of the way of the young.

Yours,

ER

Dear Sir Jeremy

Apologies for not replying to last week's Bulletin. I was struck down by a rather nasty bout of 'flu, and still feel a little below par.

The press release from the private office reported, as is now traditional, that the Queen was unable to fulfil her official duties because she was suffering from a 'slight chill'.

Is it not time to abandon this faintly absurd form of words, Sir Jeremy? I must be the only person in the country who suffers from a slight chill. No one rings into work to say they won't be coming in because a slight chill has laid them low.

Presumably the idea is to make even my illness decorous and stately, but between you and me it can be rather annoying when, as was the case last week, I was feeling absolutely dreadful.

Could you have a word with someone?

I shall be feeling less 'flu-ridden next week, I hope.

Yours,

ER

Dear Sir Jeremy

I did indeed see the portrait of Catherine. I haven't a clue about art, as you well know, but I very quickly reached the same conclusion as you did.

It's frightful! How someone with such a sweet, open face can be transformed into the dreary-looking creature with a soppy smile on her face is quite beyond me.

Then again, having hideous portraits done of one tends to go with the territory. I've frequently had to smile politely as some ghastly picture of me is unveiled. Funnily enough, the ones done since I have been rather ancient are better, but the early ones of me are universally awful.

I think it's a *good* sign that artists fail to capture Catherine's personality. Rather as I was, she's an open-air, outward-looking person. Her face, because life has been kind to her, gives little away. Openness is the one quality that defeats portrait artists.

Diana, on the other hand, was a perfect subject for them. Sweet and pretty, of course, but beyond the smile, all sorts of other, sadder stories were being told. No wonder that people loved to paint her.

It is why Catherine is so perfect for William. She is herself. The various ridiculous versions of her that 'court correspondents' come up with will bounce off her. Her late mother-in-law absorbed them. She actually took them seriously. And, of course, they infected her before long.

Simplicity is what is required. An outward look. The

courage to be your own version of yourself, and let the rest of the world go hang.

William and Catherine came to dinner not long after the portrait had been ceremoniously unveiled, and there were shrieks of laughter about it. In that quietly waggish way that he has developed since being with Catherine, William said he thought it was a rather good likeness.

His new wife pretended to be upset, and he apologised, and there was much lovey-dovey making up over the dinner table, which made the Consort look a little restless. Funnily enough,I find a young couple cosying up to one another in front of other people less irritating than it used to be.

What I like about Catherine, and what gives me *great* hope for the future, is that she takes none of it too seriously. Of course, public life *is* serious, as we all know, but to survive it all there has to be a part of you that stands aside and sees the silly side of what we do in the name of duty.

The Consort, who at one stage in his life developed an alarming interest in psychology, used to talk mysteriously about something called 'alienation'. It was unhealthy, he seemed to think, to have these two parts of one, the public and the private.

Well, I don't know much about anything, but it seems to me that, if one happens to be part of this family, a little bit of alienation can come in very handy. At the State Opening of Parliament, when I sit in the House of Lords reading the latest list of pie-in-the-sky nonsense promised by 'my government', I sometimes find myself drifting off, wondering if the dogs have been fed or whether that promising two-year-old that has been working so well at Stoute's will be good enough to win a Group One race next season.

It's not a lack of respect for my office, Sir Jeremy, simply a jolly good way to keep things in perspective. I began to learn how to keep the private and the public separate when I was quite young, during the days between my father's rather shockingly early death and the State funeral.

There was private grief and public grief, I discovered. When I was being watched by the world, I couldn't be myself. I'm beginning to hope that Catherine has learned the noble art of alienation without having to go through the really quite tricky times I had to.

I told her that she shouldn't worry about the portrait. I get pictures of me sent from around the world every day. I seem to remember a certain Sir Jeremy showing them to me, sometimes with malicious glee!

I told Catherine that some of them used to hang by the henhouse at Sandringham to scare off the foxes. They worked a treat.

Yours,

ER

D_{ear} Sir Jeremy

I'm afraid your last Bulletin made me feel rather weary!

Henry, you tell me, is in trouble again. Or rather the papers says he is. He has become their Preferred Target of the moment, just as Sarah Ferguson was a few years ago. Is there something about red hair, I wonder?

How odd it all is, though. The press say they want us to be 'human' and 'in touch with ordinary people', but the truth is they want no such thing. As soon as a PT behaves in a human or ordinary way, saying something honest or going to a party and having a glass or two too many, there is no end of a fuss.

I have come to the conclusion that people want us to be idealised, better-behaved versions of themselves. If you're young and full of vim, that can be a bit of a tall order!

Some of the family have never been able to play the game. Margaret Rose was hopeless at it, and so was Anne. Andrew and Edward are better at it than many people think, but I do worry about Henry. He has never quite grasped the fact that the public expect a certain dignified dullness from us. He has only to look to his older brother to see how that's done.

When I mentioned all this to Henry during a quiet moment at Christmas, he seemed to think I was joking. I could be a very wicked grandmother sometimes, he said.

He does make me laugh.

Y_{ours,}

ER

Dear Sir Jeremy

Thank you for your interesting thoughts on the subject of Preferred Targets. I suspect that, in your sweet and diplomatic way, you are telling me that I am talking nonsense.

'What of your gracious mother?' you ask. 'No one could accuse the Queen Mother of being dull.'

Of course not. My mother was certainly what they like to call 'a character', but she had also learned how to play the game. More than once she told me that people meeting her saw what they wanted to see. She was an image. She represented something for each of them – courage, or warmth, or humour, or good manners, or traditional Britishness. She was 'the good old Queen Mum, God bless 'er'.

As she grew older, she realised that the less she was herself, the better everything went. Sometimes that made her quite cross. She was unusually touchy about a phrase that the press started using: 'the nation's favourite grandmother'.

'What's the <u>matter</u> with people?' she used to say. 'Haven't they got their own grandmothers?'

Did I ever tell you that when she was in her eighties, my mother became rather tired of all the travelling about and having to be pleased to see every stranger she met? She developed what she called 'smile fatigue'.

So she came up with an idea. She would use a stand-in now and then.

It's true. There was this marvellous old girl from Bromsgrove. I think her name was Doris, or maybe Dot.

She made her living from one of those lookalike agencies.
She was an imitation Queen Mother, and I must say the
resemblance really was quite uncanny. We got in touch
with her and, just occasionally, when my mother wanted a
rest, Doris (or Dot) would play the part for real. No one
expected the Queen Mother to say anything to anyone on
these occasions. So Doris just smiled and waved on her
behalf while my mother was having a bit of a rest at home.
It worked out terribly well for everyone.

   I am not suggesting for a moment that I would do such a
thing, but merely making the point that it is a positive
asset not to be too human. I worry that Henry has yet to
learn that lesson.

Yours,

ER

Dear Sir Jeremy

There does seem to have been an extraordinary amount in the press about the Pope and his retirement. Of course, being the leader of a church is an important business (one understands that all too well) but in the end, he is a just a dear old man who has decided to spend his last days as a private citizen rather than a public monument.

If you look at recent popes and our family, it is like seeing two different versions of the ageing process.

We prefer to pretend that it's not happening, don't we? Look at the Consort, the way he stands and walks, the sparkle in his eyes, the need to tell dubious jokes in order to keep people on their toes. He may be old but, in the way he presents himself, he is not that different from the man he was 30 or 40 years ago.

Popes, on the other hand, have hardly taken office before they become stooped, ancient, papery and exhausted. When did you last see a pope looking the world in the eye and talking in a normal, unquavery voice? It seems to be part of the job description to look decrepit.

I wonder if it is intentional. Perhaps appearing to be of a great age confers more authority on them. Or maybe it is a way of indicating that they are nearer to heaven.

I can't help feeling that Pope Benedict isn't being slightly feeble about this. If his predecessors have been able to stay the course, I really don't see why it should be beyond him.

The Consort remarked that it was rather unGerman of him. He has a point.

Yours,

ER

Dear Sir Jeremy

Thank you for sending me the article everyone has been talking about but no one wanted to show me. I confess that the *London Review of Books* is not part of my regular reading and, having tried it, I can see why.

Are they paid by the word, these authors? Is it impossible for them to make their point in less than three extremely long, tightly printed pages? One would think that writing for a living would make one <u>more</u> concise, not less.

Nor had I heard of Hilary Mantel, although Thrusting Justin tells me she has won lots of prizes and is what he insists on calling a 'player'.

I was reluctant to read what she had written about Catherine, having heard some of her comments at second-hand through the newspapers, but to judge from the opening paragraphs of her interminable article, she was trying to be funny in the way of authors and was not in the slightest bit unsympathetic.

I confess my eyes did begin to glaze over when Mrs Mantel became rather crude in her language. It's all very well reading about what Henry VIII saw in Jane Seymour but I fail to understand the point of using unnecessary medical and sometimes smutty terms. I closed my *London Review of Books* rather sharply when I read the words, 'We have arrived at the crux of the matter: a royal lady is a royal vagina.'

Thank you very much, Mrs Mantel. That's quite enough from you.

One part of what she wrote did intrigue me, though. She claims to have had some sort of encounter with me. Although this meeting, needless to say, amounted to no more than being in the same room as me, it did ring a vague bell.

The occasion was one of the receptions we now like to hold for stalwarts of the economy – accountants, fashion designers, computer people, the 'hospitality' industry and so on. These evenings are not, it is safe to say, a high point in my social calendar. Three and a half thousand people gather in the State Rooms and pretend to look at the paintings while they gossip with one another about their own particular field.

It is always hard work, but without doubt the least enjoyable in modern memory was the one that (I assume) Mrs Mantel attended.

It was for book people – publishers, authors and so on. Harry Potter was all the rage and there was much talk of Britain's 'creative industries'. Some bright spark thought that the time had come when we would have to let the authors in.

Mrs Mantel recalls that they hung back rather than speak to me, and she is not entirely wrong. Many of them seemed uncertain as to whether they should simper or sneer. There was a lot of glancing out of the side of their eyes, and shuffling away when I approached as if being seen talking to the Queen would be bad for their reputation.

The conversations that one did have were also a bit of an uphill battle. The authors, instead of being polite and chatting about their lives as normal people do when they meet me, wanted to make an impression. Some actually asked questions, as if one was there to give them material for their books. There were inappropriate jokes. I found myself moving from one group to another rather more quickly than usual on these occasions because the standard of conversation was so poor.

Most of them just gawped at me, and that undignified group included the now-famous Mrs Mantel, it seems. I do seem to remember a lady novelist in a slightly *de trop* lobster-pink cocktail dress.

In her article, she wrote that at one moment it was as if there were only two of us in the room (people often feel like that when they meet me), and that the power of her stare made me turn to look at her.

It's possible, I suppose. If I did, I may well have been slightly annoyed at her gawping at me, but that would not have suited the book that Mrs Mantel, like every author in the State Rooms, was already writing in her head. I wore an expression of 'hurt bewilderment', she says. Apparently, this was because I had been turned into a 'thing that existed only to be looked at'.

Well, excuse me, Mrs Mantel, but who exactly is doing the looking on this occasion? And, perhaps, if I really was looking at her with 'hurt bewilderment', the usual, polite thing to do would have been to say something. It's odd how somebody with so many words at her disposal is unable to find a couple of them in order to behave like a normal human being.

That though, was not the end of it. She says in her article that the evening became 'all too much for her', and so she went behind one of the sofas and sat on the floor.

So *that* was the future star of the *London Review of Books*! I do distinctly recall, towards the end of that interminable evening, looking across the room to see what at first glance appeared to be a large wedding cake, which someone had left on the floor. On closer examination, I saw it was a guest, the lady novelist in pink, looking about her with a wondering smile on her face.

'That's a rather extraordinary sight, I must say,' I said to the Consort, who happened to be nearby.

He muttered something about 'special needs' and led me away.

Well, Mrs Mantel managed to write her story in the end and, in the way of these things, it is one that makes her look interesting and sensitive, and me a 'bewildered thing'.

I imagine there's no point in getting someone to write a firm note to this self-important magazine. Another windy three-page article would be written, and I'm not sure I could bear to be responsible for that.

Perhaps I should have a word with Mrs Mantel when she comes to collect the honour that is undoubtedly heading her way. Or perhaps not – it might be 'all too much for her' and she would have to plump herself down on the floor again.

Yours,

ER

Dear Sir Jeremy

Your report of the latest political goings-on have made me feel strangely restless. There may be a leadership challenge in the Conservatives, you say. The opposition is ahead in the polls. An entirely new party, led by that rather vulgar man with a French name, is making its presence felt.

I sense that soon yet another new face will be appearing in the library for the weekly prime ministerial meeting. The political merry-go-round seems to turn faster every year.

It is always interesting, that first meeting with a new Prime Minister. It somehow sets the pattern for those to follow. I've heard it said that, when a couple first walks out together, the seed of the relationship between them is sown, and so it is with prime ministers.

Harold Macmillan was instantly at ease, rather too familiar, between you and me; I kept expecting him to light up a cigar and tell a risqué joke. Sir Alec Douglas-Home had the look of a man who wished he was out shooting with his dog. Little Mr Wilson was somewhat cowed, with an odd posture, which made him look as if he was half-bowing all the time (perhaps he was).

And so it has continued into the modern age. Margaret Thatcher always behaved as if she had more important matters to attend to. That poor old Major chap was tongue-tied and hopeless. Mr Blair was a salesman, very smooth, like someone who had been on a course in how to appear sincere. Mr Brown was a schoolboy with ink on his hands. The Head Boy has rather too much confidence for his own good. He is a non-listener.

I listen. I smile. I try to make them feel at ease without being overfamiliar (there are some secrets of political life which I would really prefer not to know), and they, without fail, reveal more to me than they ever would to that bullying Mr Humphrys on the *Today* programme.

The Consort has said that it's because they are nervous, but I have reached the opposite conclusion.

Quite soon, each of them realises that, when they meet me, they don't have to impress me or win my vote or become friends. I am obliged to meet them, however well or badly they behave. They can be themselves.

I wonder who the next one will be.

Yours,

ER

Dear Sir Jeremy

I'm glad that the new documentary has been well received. As you know, I had my reservations about yet another 'behind the scenes at the palace' programme, but I am, of course, delighted to have been proved wrong.

Confidentially, I suspect the original problem lay in the way it was presented to me. When I was told it would be 'a royal reality show', I had my doubts about whether that was quite the way to show our family to the world. As the Consort put it, the very last thing we need around here is reality.

Still, anything for a quiet life. When, just after the Olympics, Thrusting Justin told me that they had received a 'pitch' for a new programme, I agreed at least to listen to what was proposed.

Since it would involve him, the Consort was rather grumpily present when the three media chaps did their presentation. Inevitably, it involved a 'power point'. I begin to wonder whether, soon, anyone will be able to explain something without the aid of computers and pictures flashing up on a screen.

They were pretty much what you'd expect – middle-aged men dressed as teenagers and speaking in a language neither the Consort nor I could quite understand. One of them, in the modern way, had that rather unattractive stubble, which seems to have become all the rage.

What is that all about, Sir Jeremy? It seems the most extraordinary way for men to appear, with a three-day

growth of beard on their faces. You know my opinion of
men with beards, but at least they have the courage of their
own facial hair. I remember noticing it on Charles Clarke,
the burly former Home Secretary, whom I always used to
rather like. That uncouth Sugar man on the TV has one. Is
it meant to look tough, d'you think? To me, a semi-beard
suggests someone who can't quite make up his mind, like a
man wearing a tie but keeping his top button undone.

Anyway, there they were, all stubble and linen suits,
looking nervous and laughing loudly when the Consort
made one of his waspish remarks.

I confess that I felt a little waspish, too, after their
'pitch'. They showed film footage of the family in the
1950s. Then there was the famous documentary from
1969 and a mercifully brief clip from Edward's *It's a Royal
Knockout* farrago. There were news stories from around
the world about the Queen Mother, Diana, Charles and
oneself.

At the end of it all, one of the men said that the Olympics
had been what he called 'a game changer'. My appearance
with James Bond had shown my 'human side', he said (how
many times does my human side have to be shown before
the penny drops that I am actually human, I wonder?).
Apparently, my jumping out of a helicopter had caused a
'paradigm shift in public perception of the Royals'.

At about this stage, there was a low volcanic rumble
emanated from beside me, and I began to worry that the
Consort was going to have one of his turns. There's only a
certain amount of this kind of stuff that he can take.

I remarked to the three pitchers that I was glad my James

Bond film had gone down so well. But, I wondered, was there really a need for yet another documentary?

They looked slightly nervous. Then one of them, with much throat-clearing and hopping from one foot to the other, said that the Olympics film had shown that the royal 'brand' needed to be 'refreshed'.

Aware that the Consort and I were looking at him somewhat coldly, the man added that there was nothing wrong with a royal brand. It was the best way of presenting the right image of the family to the outside world. These days, he said, the most successful public figures (he mentioned some names of people I've never heard of, presumably of pop or film stars) liked to refresh their personal brand once every few months.

The stubbly man added that these people were known in the publicity business as 'brandividuals'.

The Consort gave a rumbling growl.

In a way, said the first man, ploughing on bravely, the consummate brandividual of the past half-century was none other than the Queen Mother.

Beside me, the Consort stirred.

'More like a gindividual, as I recall,' he muttered, causing much simpering laughter among the pitchers.

In the end, there is no resisting these things. The film-maker seemed to be perfectly harmless, and it was agreed that we would have the chance to look through the film and take out anything we disliked.

Talking about it later, the Consort and I agreed that, like other behind-the-scenes films, it would be described as 'unprecedented' and 'revolutionary' but would be nothing of the kind.

One has to go along with these faintly pointless films to keep the staff happy and to give the impression that we are in touch. Everyone has to be in touch these days, don't they? Or at least give that impression.

The newspaper reaction has shown that we were right. There has been much favourable comment about a particular conversation I had with the Head Boy at one of our weekly meetings. A clip of my ankles beneath the desk during the Christmas broadcast seems to have caused much excitement.

I mean, honestly, Sir Jeremy, could anything be sillier?

It is my sincere hope that our 'brand' has been sufficiently 'refreshed' to keep these people away from us at least for a few months.

Yours,

ER

D ear Sir Jeremy

Was it my imagination or was the inauguration of the new Archbishop of Canterbury somewhat *piano*, as my sister used to say?

Perhaps it was because a new Pope has been elected recently, and nothing we do, thank goodness, can compete with that theatrical nonsense (the locked door, the puffs of smoke, the speeches in Latin to thousands of thoroughly overexcited 'believers'). It seems to me that there's something a bit pagan about it all.

Our way is to have a few prayers, a quick 'The Lord is My Shepherd' and off you go. I know which one I prefer.

On the other hand, I can't help feeling that the Catholics have the right idea when it comes to names. They understand that a person's title is important. The new chap may be Julio (or whatever) from Buenos Aires but, in order to win over the reverent millions around the world, he must take on the name of a 13th-century saint and become Pope Francis.

Of course, one could take this too far, but I do wonder whether our own church might not 'refresh' its 'brand' in the same way. I mean, Justin Welby: who is going to fall on his knees in front of someone who sounds like a hairdresser?

They tell me he was once in the oil business, which makes a change. No doubt his term will be all very different from the way it was with the Williams chap, who always seemed like a bright but rather unhappy teacher.

My conversations with Dr Williams never went terribly well, between you and me. They became as tangled and confused as his beard. The last time I saw him, I wondered, quite innocently, whether God was sending us this awful weather to remind us that we should take care of the planet on which He has put us.

The Archbishop looked most uncomfortable. There was much tugging of the beard and running of fingers through the hair and sucking of teeth and crossing and uncrossing of legs.

'I'm not irrevocably convinced that, in what one might call the general scheme of things, that is the model to which we are essentially adhering,' he said eventually.

Goodness. That took a bit of unscrambling, as you can imagine. More out of politeness than anything else (if the Defender of the Faith cannot ask these things, who can?), I asked which part of the 'model' was the problem.

He sent over another barrage of utter meaninglessness.

I gave him the Look, and he writhed around a bit more. To tell the truth, I was slightly annoyed that a perfectly harmless remark about God and the weather had proved to be so controversial.

'Is God the problem?' I asked. 'Is it that you don't think God's responsible for the weather?'

There was a theatrical wince behind the great beard.

'God, good, let's not get mired in the semantics,' he said, like a man trying to make things simple for a rather dim pupil. 'There is a force. Let us call it the Latin term "*virtus*", or to quote Hamlet . . .'

And off he went again into the dark thickets of his mind.

I decided not to follow him. Frankly, if you have an Archbishop of Canterbury who sees no difference between God and good, then the whole business becomes a bit of a waste of time.

A man who's embarrassed by the idea of a Creator in charge of the weather is hardly likely to lead his flock down the path of righteousness. I reached the conclusion some time ago that the more a person thinks, the less he leads. Hesitation is in his soul.

Having an open mind is all very well in civilian life but, when it comes to being in charge of a church or a country, it can look remarkably like weakness. I've seen it in politicians. As soon as I met Michael Foot, a sweet, slightly shambolic man, whose head was clearly full of ideas bumping and jostling against one another, I knew that he would never be a real success. Dr Williams is a church version of Mr Foot.

The archbishops who have seemed to me best suited to the job have not been thinkers, like Dr Williams, nor eager executives, like Archbishop Justin with his bright salesman's eyes. They were more like elderly uncles, good-hearted souls, who would lurk around benignly at important occasions. Fisher, Coggan, Runcie – even their names sound reliable and English.

They wouldn't <u>dream</u> of mentioning God in conversation. It would be the most <u>appallingly</u> bad form. As far as they were concerned, there was no point in fretting about what He is or does. He just exists. That's all we need to know. In fact, He is like the most marvellous all-powerful Uncle himself.

Maybe it is old-fashioned, this idea that there is a God, that He is kind and above all earthly things, and, if we do our best to obey His Commandments, He will make sure that our reward is in the next world, but I must say, it has always worked for me. I just know He is there all round us. He is in the gentle eye of a horse, the trust of a dog, in the trees one is forever planting at ceremonies all over the country.

I do worry about now having a dynamic Archbishop of Canterbury. He'll have an agenda, 'action points'. Committees will be set up. He'll want to get things done.

Does God really want us to be dynamic problem-solvers? Somehow, I suspect not.

Yours,

ER

Dear Sir Jeremy

I'm surprised that my reference to 'the Look' confused you. You've been around for so long that I always assume you're familiar with our little professional secrets.

The Look is simply a tip passed on from generation to generation in my family. It is a way we have of expressing displeasure without wasting time or energy on words. When a conversation is straying into areas that are unwelcome, or is simply becoming too dull to be borne any longer, we use the Look. As the Consort says, it could bring down a stag from a range of 50 yards.

I learned the Look from my Uncle David, who in turn had been coached by his father, George V. My attempts to pass it on to the children have met with varying success.

Of course, some of us are better at it than others. Margaret liked to think she had the Look but the awful truth is it just made her look rather peevish. She never quite mastered the knack of bringing the social temperature down to below zero in the blink of an eye.

Anne was a natural. In fact, her ex-husband Mark's only known witticism was that she was actually born with the Look. Charles had to be taught and eventually, after much practice over Christmas dinner and so on, can now carry it off reasonably well.

The others never really mastered it. Andrew looks as if he's eaten something nasty and when Teddy Edward has a go at it, no one notices.

Of course, it doesn't always work. Americans, for example, seem utterly impervious to it.

I once gave President Bush the full works at a state dinner when he was halfway through an off-colour story about breeding techniques on a bloodstock farm in Texas. He ploughed on, as pleased with himself as ever, chuckling away at his own smuttiness, completely ignoring the Look. Funnily enough, I had the same problem when the Clinton man, who, mid-conversation, actually laid a hand on my arm and (I still can't quite believe this) squeezed.

I'm slightly concerned about the grandchildren, neither of whom seem as keen to learn the Look as one might have hoped. William says he is worried about what he calls 'the negative PR aspect' while Henry is openly rebellious.

'But, Granny, why should I actually want to look like a grumpy old sod?' he asked me not so long ago.

'Because, dear Henry,' I might have answered (but decided not to), 'it is part of your duty. Words, as you should know better than most, can be dangerous. The Look is a way of exerting authority (avoiding embarrassment, if you prefer) without laying oneself open to criticism or unnecessarily hurting people's feelings.' I expect he'll learn it one day.

I'll give you a demonstration of how it works when you're next here, Sir Jeremy. You'll need a stiff drink to recover.

Yours,

ER

Dear Sir Jeremy

Thank you for sending me a CD of Charles's appearance on the *Countryfile* programme. I always enjoy *Countryfile*, in spite of its rather annoying presenters, but I must confess that, when I heard that Charles was one, I found myself catching up on the Sunday papers that evening.

Much as I love him, I have never thought that appearing on TV was his strong point. He always seems rather too eager to be amusing (or serious). But he was fine, wasn't he?

These days it's probably a good thing for a future monarch to be seen out and about, doing things.

I was surprised to feel rather moved to see him there, surrounded by the ingratiating Matt, the girl and the man who used to be on Children's Hour. Something happens to men in their sixties, I've noticed. There's a sort of re-connection with themselves as boys. They have been through life's various nonsenses, and they've been daddies and bosses and have had their share of knocks and disappointments, and now that they've reached the home straight, they can stop trying so hard. They can become boys again. It's why school reunions happen at that age. They are all entering a secret, dignified (with some exceptions, admittedly) second childhood.

Seeing Charles hacking away at a sapling in the touching belief that he was showing how it should be done (he's convinced that he is 'good with his hands' – I believe it's quite a joke among the gardening staff at Highgrove), I was reminded of how he was all those years ago, when he was at his prep school at Cheam.

He was always a tremendous tryer. He knew it was his duty to be brave, not to cry at the beginning of term, to be keen on sports, to put the masters at their ease, to be polite and grown-up even though he was only seven. One day he would be king. People who are going to be king don't blub when saying goodbye to their parents.

We had to make a big decision about where to send him after Cheam and, Sir Jeremy, I still wonder, to this day, whether we got it right. It was a very male world in those days and although fathers wouldn't dream of being involved in the bringing up of children, there was one area in which they expected to have the first and last word: where boys should go to school.

I had always assumed that Charles would go to Eton. It was a perfectly good school, handy for Windsor, and knew how to look after the sons of those in the public eye. I liked the sort of chap the school seemed to turn out. Old Etonians can be a little full of themselves sometimes (think of the Head Boy and man with the scruffy hair who is Mayor of London) but I have always thought that was a fault on the right side.

Rough edges can be knocked off. It is the edgeless who are the problem. But there was a general feeling about the place that Charles lacked a certain toughness when he was at Cheam. He was rather keener on reading books than one might wish for a boy of ten or eleven and would wander around the garden, looking at the flowers. Observing his son, the Consort would occasionally use a word that one rarely hears these days.

'I couldn't bear it if the boy turned out to be *wet*,' he said.

Needless to say, the various men who were there to advise me all the time, all of whom had been to public school, took the same line, even the wet ones (particularly the wet ones!). What a disaster it would be, they all said, if Charles emerged from Eton a limp-wristed, misty-eyed bookworm. It would be too late to give him a backbone at that stage.

Gordonstoun was very sound on general attitude, the Consort said. It would be the making of Charles. I had to agree that, if my husband was a typical old boy, there was unlikely to be a wetness problem.

So off Charles went. The Queen Mother objected but even she was pretty much ignored. What do women know about how a chap should be educated? We hadn't been in dorms, or gone for cross-country runs, or been flicked with towels in the showers. The fact that I had never been to a school of any sort rather weakened my position.

I remember going to see Charles playing a game of rugger at Gordonstoun when he was about 14. He was in his house's Second XV and, because he's never been very fast, the poor chap was in the scrum, which he clearly hated.

At first, I thought I was imagining it – the way the other boys crashed into him, threw him down in the mud and piled in on top of him every time he had the ball. I glanced at the Consort. The fixed smile on his face told me that he was noticing it, too.

'Very good,' he said now and then. 'Well played.'

In a way, the men were right. When he emerged after his A-levels, Charles did seem rather more <u>flinty</u> than he had been. He had learned how important it was to be tough, and from then on he was always game to try anything – climbing mountains, riding in point-to-points, swimming in rivers, dancing the twist. It sometimes ended in tears (I've never known anyone quite so loose in the saddle!) but at least he had a go. Down the years, he has shown his father, and the world, that he is certainly not wet.

During the period, not so long ago, when he was (his phrase) 'talking to someone', he started using an entirely new vocabulary. Speaking of William when he was in his early teens, Charles described him as 'a pleaser'. Apparently, it's not such a good thing as one might imagine to be a pleaser. You are 'less-in-touch with yourself', Charles said. You lack 'self-validation'.

But, of course, a pleaser is exactly what Charles has always been. He wants to fit in, to please those around him at any particular time.

So he pleased as a naval officer, then (rather unconvincingly) as a man-about-town, then (even worse) as part of a glamorous celebrity couple. He tried to please that rather odd Van der Post man and became a wise environmentalist. Now, thanks to Camilla, he is a country gent, laying his hedges, pleasing himself.

And pleasing is exactly what is needed now. It has taken 65 years but dear Charles is becoming himself at just the right time. There is such a thing as too much confidence in a monarch. The nation wants a pleaser.

I think Charles can see that, too. He looks at ease with himself, almost for the first time in his life. It is going to turn out well for my son, the pleaser-king, and that makes me very happy.

Yours,

ER

Dear Sir Jeremy

I have absolutely no idea what you mean when you say you
detect a 'sub-text' in my last letter. I was simply 'sharing',
as Diana used to say. I hope I was not <u>oversharing</u>, as she
could sometimes do.

Just because I say that Charles is now in perfect shape to
take my place, it doesn't mean that I have an eye on the
door marked 'exit'. I admit that the dignified retirement of
Queen Beatrix and the rather more shambolic departure of
Pope Benedict have caused my imagination to wander into
a future when I am not at the centre of things, though.

Think of Beatrix and Benedict now, Sir Jeremy. The
moment they are no longer this great thing in the eyes
of the world, they will be allowed simply to potter about,
two old people, thinking their thoughts, moving at their
own speed, with no care or interest in whether their
'brand' needs to be 'refreshed', or how they are going
to appear to billions of strangers almost every day of
their lives.

The bliss of it all! What almost everyone else takes for
granted, the freedom to be their private selves, is to me a
distant dream. Sometimes, the longing to be left alone, to
be invisible to strangers, is an almost physical ache.

A couple of Christmases ago, I was talking to my
grandson Henry about some ridiculous story about him
that had appeared in the papers. 'Surely, one's allowed a bit
of down-time now and then, Granny,' he said.

I had never heard the phrase 'down-time' before (it's rather good) but that is precisely what one is never allowed. I am on up-time, around the clock.

It is wearying sometimes, Sir Jeremy. You know that feeling – after a big family gathering (Christmas, perhaps) when everyone has gone, one feels slightly wrung out by all that affection and warmth and smiling. Now imagine that the family is the whole world and that Christmas is every day of the year. That's what it's like.

Of course it's a pleasure to see the joy on people's faces, the way they look at you greedily as if they need to hold on to this moment for the rest of their lives, but it is tiring, too. One loses something of oneself in the process.

And, do you know, I rather think this neediness of people is getting worse. In the old days, there was a distance between us and the ordinary world. We were in the head-lines or (if one was called Margaret Rose) in the gossip columns. Now and then, one appeared on the television news. Now, because everyone has become so addicted to their little screens, we are there all the time.

I can't help wondering whether it is not getting out of hand. You might have heard that, after my Olympics film with James Bond, something rather peculiar happened on one of the Pacific Islands (I honestly can't remember which one).

After they had watched the opening ceremony on TVs in the local bars, they began to believe that this Queen of England, who jumped out of a helicopter and into the Olympic Games, might do the same on their island. Tremendous excitement erupted whenever a new helicopter appeared. Crowds gathered, people jumped up and down pointing to the heavens, expecting The Great White Queen Who Comes From The Sky to float down to pay them a visit.

And we are not so different here. A story in one of the French magazines during the 1990s reported that Diana had *'la puissance royale'* (the royal touch) with which she could cure disease. Charles, who loves to look these things up on the internet, told me that this dates back to the Middle Ages, when people used to believe that the royal touch could cure scrofula.

I see this madness myself in the eyes of those I meet. They gaze at me, they want to be close, they want to touch me as if my very presence has some kind of almost holy power to change things.

One gets used to it (the trick is to be somewhere else in one's mind), but it takes its toll, this strange and desperate expectation that there is something more to us than flesh and blood.

Recently, you know, a new problem has developed at royal receptions and honours ceremonies. Once or twice a month, some member of the public is so overcome by the occasion that, at the moment when one meets them, they lose control of their bladders. I have learned to move on, smile in place, and a mop is quickly on the scene. But it is strange, isn't it, people reacting to me rather as my young bitch Cherry would react when one of the gamekeepers' Labradors bounded up to her and gave her a fright? She was so overcome that she just let go.

Can you wonder that now, without too much longer on this earth, I've begun to secretly hanker for a rest? Just as

Diana used to overshare, I have been overloved, overrevered. I look at Charles and see a man who is ready for all this. He wouldn't mind people wetting themselves when they meet him. He'd probably rather like it.

I'm thoroughly fed up with this ghastly weather, aren't you? We all deserve a jolly good spring.

Yours,

ER

Dear Sir Jeremy

I must confess that I thought the lead item in your latest
Bulletin was an early April Fool. The Johnson chap as the
next Prime Minister? Surely someone's having a joke at our
expense.

I watched the TV programme on him the other night, as
instructed by you, and confess I am none the wiser. I'm
sure he's frightfully amusing (he reminds me a bit of
Andrew when he's on form) but to think of him leading his
country, or even his party, is something my poor old
imagination simply isn't up to.

At this stage in one's life, there is a tendency to see the
child in people. I look at someone apparently grown-up and
in charge of this or that, and I see a schoolboy (this works
less well with women, I find) still unable to believe that he
is getting away with it.

It began to happen about 20 years ago. When John Major
first appeared, he seemed to be like a middle-order member
of the sixth form, rather uneasily aware that he was lucky
to be senior prefect. Then there was Mr Blair, the bright
boy who would do anything to be popular, followed by
Mr Brown, the swot, and Mr Cameron, the head boy who
had known where he would end up from the moment he
arrived at school.

Now, if you and others are to be believed, it is the school
joker who will one day be bouncing into the library with
that rather pleased-with-himself smile on his face.

The Consort has always believed that hair is a great indicator of character, and he may be right. One glance at Michael Foot and one knew that he would never be Prime Minister. Too shaggy by half. Then there was Mr Heseltine – what on earth did he do to himself to get that great beehive of hair on his head? Whatever it was, it must have taken a lot of effort and self-love.

Never trust a man who spends too much time on his hair, Sir Jeremy. It is one of life's more reliable rules. When Heseltine was Secretary of State for Defence, a photograph of him visiting the troops appeared in the press. He had on a trim combat jacket, which seemed to have been very carefully ironed, and some expensive Jermyn Street desert boots, and wore a coiffure that seemed to be living a life of its own. What did he think he looked like?

The Johnson man seems to have the opposite problem, forever ruffling his rather vulgar blond locks as if worried that he'll look too smart, but it comes down to the same thing in the end, I fear. Male vanity. Profoundly unattractive in my view. I mean, if you can't control your hair, what chance have you got of controlling the country?

The other evening when we were at Sandringham, I wandered into the drawing room, having finished my boxes. The Consort was sitting bolt upright in his usual chair, watching a documentary about the National Health Service. Every time a new interviewee appeared on the screen, he said, 'Get your hair cut.'

I asked him if he was actually watching the programme.

'Get your hair cut!' he said. 'Get your hair cut!'

He was right in a way. It was odd how many of the men,

important enough to be interviewed for a TV programme, were just slightly scruffy when it came to their hairstyle.

I tried to get the Consort to snap out of it. 'That one's not too bad, surely?' I said.

'Get your hair cut!'

In the end, I had to leave him to it. I dread to think what he will have to say if he has to meet the school joker.

Yours,

ER

Dear Sir Jeremy

I've read your explanation of what is going on in the Euro-zone and am not, I fear, very much the wiser. All I know is that every night on the news for weeks now, there are olive-skinned men and women looking worried, tearful or angry.

Is it my imagination or is early 21st-century news rather different from late 20th-century news? All those accents! Suddenly, what's going on in the Middle East feels as familiar as if it were happening at our back door. It's the new Northern Ireland.

Could that be the problem, I wonder? When poor old John Major droned on about EU this, Brussels that, Euro-zone the other, I would occasionally ask whether this urgent need to be <u>hugger-mugger</u> with other countries was entirely sensible.

We're different. Perhaps if you're an internationally minded Eurocrat working in an air-conditioned skyscraper in Brussels, you can believe that a wizened old chap selling olives in a marketplace in Cyprus is every bit as European as a pasty-faced teenager working on a supermarket till in Stockport, and they have this tremendous EU-bond in common, but the rest of us know that's nonsense.

One only has to look at European leaders to see how different we are. Try to imagine, Sir Jeremy, that ridiculous little Signor Berlusconi being in charge of Britain or Germany. Yet they rather liked him in Italy. Personally, he made me feel a touch nervous and even the Consort, who likes nothing better than salty man-talk, looked uneasy when the Italian took him aside at our reception with what he called 'a leedle story!' When I asked Philip about it later, he said it was about rather peculiar Italian parties (bunga-bunga, could it have been?). I was none the wiser.

If the Italians liked having this funny old man, with his dyed hair and roaming eyes, in charge of their country, that was fine by me. I was simply glad that he was not our Prime Minister. A weekly audience alone with that old goat would be distinctly unnerving.

Surely one only has to look at Signor Berlusconi and then that competent if slightly dreary Angela Merkel to see that any idea of a 'European Union' is something of a non-starter. One somehow can't imagine Frau Merkel going to a bunga-bunga party, can one?

And, of course, no one really wants to be a Euro-citizen. We're different. It's what makes us human. People take pride in their village, or town, or country. The very idea of being a Euro-citizen would feel like some sort of invasion.

One of the least thrilling moments of last year was something called the Sovereign Monarchs' Jubilee Lunch. It should have been fun – Queen Beatrix was there, full of beans as usual, and Queen Margrethe of Denmark. The King of Jordan can be surprisingly good company. The great thing about being among other royal families is that we can all relax in the knowledge that everyone knows how to behave, without the slightest hint of Berlusconi-type awkwardness.

Yet strangely, it was all rather hard work. The problem with a conversation between two monarchs is that they are both used to half-listening and murmuring polite remarks now and then. On this occasion, one became aware that two people nodding at one another and saying 'How interesting' wasn't going to work, conversationally. Someone had to lead the dance.

Of course, there is family chat with some of them, and a few have their pet subjects. One only has to mention yachting to King Constantine and he'll be talking for ten minutes.

But the others! What exactly does one say to Prince Hans-Adam of Liechtenstein, or the King of Romania, or the Crown Prince of Yugoslavia? As far as I can see, their lives are spent drifting about the place, distinguished yet obscure, doing nothing in particular but waiting dolefully for the call to return to their rightful throne. They speak, rather sadly, of their jubilees or national days, but one just knows that those occasions consist of a few old men with medals standing to attention to a tape-recording of some long-forgotten anthem.

We may all have similar titles but we are gloriously different. If some of the sovereigns worked as hard as I do, they would fade away within days. If I led the life some of them lead, I'd <u>die</u> of boredom.

It's the same with this infernal Eurozone. People should be allowed to make their own muddles, and find their own solutions, without a bossy directive from a European bureaucrat who believes that the world would be a happier place if we could all behave in exactly the same way.

Yours,

ER

Dear Sir Jeremy

Much earnest thought is being given here to the need for me to 'slow down', with action plans (or should that be inaction plans?) and meetings and talk of phases one and two. Explaining it all with his usual clarity, Thrusting Justin told me they were simply drilling down into a game-plan to take me more out of the loop, going forward. I think he was trying to tell me that my schedule is being reduced.

I can't say that the prospect of less travel perturbed me, but I must confess I have quietly resisted attempts to cut down my visits to places over here.

The truth is, I like opening things. Going to factories and watching stuff come off an enormous production-line still interests me. Living as I do in a world of talk, with politicians, diplomats, civil servants and advisers of every hue jabbering at me all day, I find it rather restful and reassuring to go to places where people actually make useful or enjoyable products, which the rest of us need.

Quite often, things go wrong, and that adds to my enjoyment. I pull a ribbon and nothing happens, or someone arrives late for an important reception, or a 21-gun salute becomes a 20-gun salute because something gets jammed. Tremendous fun. I hate too much efficiency.

I found myself thinking about how I would miss these visits this very week while touring a chocolate factory. It was one of those days when everything went to plan. There was a general air of happiness. In many ways, it was identical to countless other visits I have made down the decades, with tongue-tied executives, much shaking of hands, a woman who feels she has to keep explaining things to me however blindingly obvious they happen to be, and little clumps of employees staring bashfully and smiling at me as I make my rounds.

But it was so much fun, the chocolate tour. At every turn, we were offered samples. It was just a matter of time before the Consort made the inevitable remark.

'Don't you all get terribly fat?' he asked in a booming voice. As it happened, there were a few people who were on the portly side and so the laughter at his joke was slightly muted, I thought.

In the factory, two of the senior chocolate-makers were introduced to us, and presented a carriage made out of differently coloured chocolates, toffee and liquorice. It had taken them seven days to make. Perhaps I'm becoming a little sentimental in my old age, but I did find the idea of these two strapping men working lovingly on a little carriage made out of sweets strangely touching.

What a perfect way to earn a living, making chocolate for us all to enjoy! The Consort and I returned to Windsor, weary, smelling faintly of Mars bars, but content. It was the sort of day that I would miss dreadfully if I were 'grounded'.

Yours,

ER

Dear Sir Jeremy

It was tactful of you to mention that grim annual event, the publication of the *Sunday Times* 'Rich List', without referring to the fact that I have, I am told, risen in the 'charts' over the past year.

I know this because there was some talk in the press office as to whether what they call 'a PR offensive' is required. They are worried that, in these straitened times, the family might be seen as 'fat cats'. Apparently, it is terrible to be thought a 'fat cat' these days.

I told them in no uncertain terms that what I really regarded as offensive was even allowing such a distasteful subject to be discussed in the public arena. As you know, I am not fond of cats (devious, selfish creatures not fit to tie the bootstraps of a decent dog), nor am I well disposed to obesity, but it's the sheer <u>vulgarity</u> of the whole thing that I find depressing.

When did the world become so fascinated by the dull, private matter of how much money a person has? There was a time when no one particularly cared.

There were millionaires, like Howard Hughes and Paul Getty (usually American and almost always rather peculiar in some way or other) but, apart from them, the capital people happened to have, or the salary they might or might not be earning, was a matter for them and their stock-brokers, but nobody else.

It's a sort of sickness, in my view. Producing a whole

magazine of rich people and solemnly totting up how much they have in their bank accounts is not only the worst kind of gossip but it makes <u>everyone</u> discontented. Only a fool would be pleased to be included in the list, and those who are not are made to feel resentful and (such is human nature) jealous.

We're in the most frightful muddle about money these days. On the one hand, we blame the 'fat cats' for virtually everything that has gone wrong in the world. On the other, we pore over their bank balances and property portfolios, and rank them in a 'Rich List' as if they are moneyed gods and ordinary people should be in awe of them.

I can't help feeling that this new preoccupation with cash has caused many of the difficulties in which we find ourselves. Everybody wants more of it than they need. Even when they give it away to good causes, on Big Red Nose Day or whatever it's called, there has to be a grand circus about it. Then there are those appalling TV programmes featuring greedy young people, and usually involving that unpleasant man Sugar who doesn't shave and at the end of each programme points his stubby finger at someone and tells them, 'You're fired.'

It has become an obsession, like what I call the bed business in the 1960s. A sort of madness overcomes people and everything somehow becomes unbalanced. I used to feel slightly guilty that no one in the family is what they call 'good with money'. It's always been assumed that, as a subject of conversation, it was like discussing one's private medical matters. Now, everyone has to be weighed in the scales of cash. No one cares about what Mr Blair is doing these days, only how much money he is making.

And those bonuses, Sir Jeremy! I simply don't understand how it is that these people who are already doing very nicely thank-you still require extra millions every year. What do they spend it on? Even in photographs, there is something dead about their eyes. One can just tell that they have long forgotten how to enjoy life.

Please, when the next ghastly 'Rich List' appears, I would be grateful if you made absolutely no mention of it in your Bulletin.

Y ours,

ER

Dear Sir Jeremy

Your latest was well-timed, arriving as it did while the honours season is in full swing. Of all my duties, I must confess that spending most of a day handing out medals to worthy citizens of the realm is not the most thrilling.

It's not rewarding some battered old headteacher or a stalwart of some charity or other that I find tedious, but those at the top of the list, the oily civil servants or some 'much-loved' star of stage and screen. And when some spruced-up chief executive approaches me with the mock-humble expression people favour on these occasions, I sometimes find it difficult not to burst out laughing at the silliness of it all.

Forgive me, Sir Jeremy – I had a peculiarly tiresome day yesterday and I'm what Sarah Ferguson used to call 'venting'. Looking on the bright side, at least this year's list didn't have one of those well-heeled left-wing play-wrights who has spent a lifetime chuntering on about privilege and injustice and then cheerfully accepts a knight-hood. When one of these noble rebels kneels before me, I am often tempted to bring down the sword rather more sharply on his shoulder than usual in the hope that he might sense that one person at least has not been fooled.

Now you tell me that there is much discussion about who should be de-honoured. As a nation, we do seem to like the idea of someone being <u>stripped</u> of their knighthood.

It has a nice ring of ritual to it – stripped in front of the whole school!

Maybe we should go along with the new mood for revenge and introduce a de-honouring at which the villains of the moment – greedy bankers, disgraced disc-jockeys – would have to return shame-faced to the palace in order to hand back their medals to someone suitably severe. I nominate Anne – she was <u>born</u> for the job.

I'm grateful to you for sparing me details of the latest stories about old 'disc jockeys' and what they did 40 or 50 years ago. Am I right in thinking that some of them were involved in Teddy Edward's *It's a Royal Knockout* folly? I can't say I'm surprised.

I heard someone on the radio arguing that many of the ghastly things that happened back then reflected the 'let-it-all-hang-out' attitude of a certain generation.

Well, quite. Without wishing to be in the slightest bit smug, I have to say that, even at the time, I thought that there was something not quite right about how people suddenly started behaving in the 1960s and 1970s.

Was it called 'flower power'? We had remarkably little contact with all that, of course, but I do remember that Charles went through a slightly peculiar phase when he was at Cambridge. Not drugs or girls (he has always been very sensible in those areas) but his politics became a bit odd. When he was at Trinity, some of the students were going through what the Consort calls 'the revolting stage'. Charles would try to explain to us why they were 'sitting in' or going on a 'demo'.

He would slightly worry us sometimes. 'We should take

time to smell the flowers,' he told us on one occasion. Another time, when the Queen Mother asked him what he planned to do after university, he replied that he was going to 'get his head together' and 'do his thing'.

It was nothing too serious. His hair remained short (the Lord be praised), he never wore jeans, and his favourite pastime while at Cambridge was beagling. He did, briefly, and painfully, play the guitar. As far as I recall, he managed just one tune, which he played again and again, an endless dirge with many, many verses called 'Where Have All the Flowers Gone?'

The Consort, who has never had time for music unless it's played by a band of guards, became distinctly tetchy when he heard, Charles droning this tune.

'Not the bloody flour again,' he would groan. 'What is it, some kind of baker's lament?'

'Not *flour*, flowers, Daddy,' said Charles, in the rather gratingly soft voice he had recently started using. 'It's a protest song.'

The Consort muttered something about how a bit of fertiliser would bring back the flowers.

'The flowers are a metaphor,' said Charles primly. 'It's really about war.'

Well, that didn't go down terribly well, as you can imagine. Charles was told that, unless he dropped this hippie nonsense sharpish, he would find himself out of Cambridge and in the army. The guitar soon fell out of favour.

It was really rather a childish time, wasn't it? We kept on hearing that it was time for the new generation to have a say, but everything about those people, from their clothes to their songs and their politics, belonged to the nursery.

I admit that the 1950s were slightly stuffy, and that things needed a bit of a shake-up, but how silly it all was. Now and then, one had to meet the disc-jockeys who had suddenly become famous and important. They were like bad circus clowns. Even the ones who seemed slightly less odd had ridiculous names, like 'Stewpot' and 'the Hairy Cornflake'.

Humans, I've always thought, are rather like animals when it comes to self-control in their private lives. If one of my dogs has sex on his mind and gets into the habit of going on a bit of a ramble to find a bitch that is in an interesting condition, he will quite soon be thinking of nothing else. So it was with people in the Sixties. They lost the habit of controlling themselves – of being grown-up, really.

I fear that people still behave badly – many people never recovered that self-control and, like my old dogs, are never to be entirely trusted unless they are locked away in a kennel or castrated. I sometimes think that that approach would not be such a terrible idea with certain humans.

Yours,

ER

Dear Sir Jeremy

How astute of you to notice that the press have been in a great state of excitement about a couple of horses having to be put down at Aintree while virtually ignoring the death of some luckless boxer from injuries to his head.

People do so love to pretend that the British care about animals, don't they?

I've always thought that treatment of animals was a simple matter. God put us on this earth to exist with his creatures. Animals give us food and company and sport. In return, we should respect and be kind to them, but once people get the idea into their heads that humans and animals should have the same rights, they are going to get into the most terrible muddle.

Surely, it's perfectly obvious that if it's cruel to put a horse down when it breaks a leg racing, then it's also cruel to make them race one another for our amusement. By the same argument, they shouldn't be made to jump things or go in and out of poles in a bending race at a gymkhana, either.

None of these things are natural but, since time began, horses have earned their keep by working in our fields, carrying our soldiers, pulling our carriages and giving us fun. If they hadn't been useful to us, they would not be here, or they would be curiosities in a game park, like a zebra or a gazelle. Is that what these people want? No bloodstock, no racing, no equestrian sports?

And what about other things? It's not exactly kind to keep a budgerigar in a cage or goldfish in a bowl, and think of those millions of hamsters, allowed out of their cages only to be mauled by children.

Maybe I'm out of touch but it seems to me that the more everyone talks about cruelty to animals, the more cruelty there is. When I mentioned those unfortunate horses being sent abroad for slaughter in some ghastly knackers yard in the Ukraine to the Head Boy, he got himself into the most awful tangle.

It was all very difficult, he managed to blurt out in the end. There were European regulations. He was considering setting up an enquiry (a sure sign that nothing more will be heard of it).

Did you watch the National? Rather fun, although like everyone else I was rather hoping the Irish girl would win. That's the kind of 'feminism' I support.

I sometimes think that it was the Grand National which helped influence my life. It was not just that quite extra-ordinary moment in 1956 when poor old Devon Loch launched himself into the air 40 yards from the post and then did the splits. It was what followed.

No one was a more devoted supporter of racing than the Queen Mother, and here, until that moment, was her beloved horse about to achieve her greatest ambition as an owner.

I was standing with Margaret Rose beside her as Devon Loch passed the Elbow. The sound of the crowd was quite deafening. When it happened, there was a brief silence, then this great groan as ESB galloped past. It was almost biblical, Sir Jeremy.

The Queen Mother reached for me, and held my arm tightly. Then, before anyone else, she recovered herself.

'Are they all right?' she asked. 'Is he lame?' As Dick Francis stood there, a lonely miserable figure in the centre of the course, she murmured, 'Poor Francis. What a thing to happen.'

You see? Immediately she was thinking of other people. We went down to see the trainer, Peter Cazalet, and Dick Francis, who was rather tearful about the whole thing. The lad trotted Devon Loch up and no harm seemed to have been done. Later, I believe she wrote to him to say how proud she was of the stable. As far as she was concerned, she said, it would always be Devon Loch's National.

Winning was not the thing for her. The race, the horse, the connections were what mattered. And because she was so graceful about it all, it was better for everyone else. She showed them, and us (me, in particular) that it was <u>futile</u> to be too competitive. Fun was what mattered.

Some people think that's a weakness, but I don't. Whenever there have been disappointments in life, a temptation to become thoroughly ill-tempered about a bit of bad luck, two words have managed to keep me smiling through: Devon Loch.

But that was it, as far as jumping was concerned. From then on, I was a flat girl. The Queen Mother loved the cold and the wet and the crashing falls, and the whole mud-splattered madness of steeplechasing but, after that day in March 1956, I knew that my enthusiasm would be for the flat.

I like the breeding side, the way that quality is more important than luck. It's smoother and smarter than jump-racing (you can't love them both equally) and that was what I preferred.

Did you back the winner? 66–1! I fear you may have been listening to one of your classical records rather than watching the race. I have fond memories of the year you came to Royal Ascot with us, somewhat reluctantly. When you said that one of the horses in the paddock had 'ants in its pants', we all knew that, when it came to racing, you were beyond hope.

Yours,

ER

Dear Sir Jeremy

Of course, you are right. With the approaching event, the attention of the press will once more be in the direction of the Middletons.

I do sometimes wonder why the world is so fascinated by the idea that a straightforward, 'civilian' family can become a semi-attached member of our own rather different set-up. No doubt the usual ridiculous fuss will be made over the fact that, many years ago, Carole was once an air-hostess.

As I grow older, I become more and more convinced that few things in life are more futile and lowering than class snobbery. Every few years or so, we are told that we are now a classless society (as if that were a wonderful thing in itself) but, when I look around, it seems to me that class is more on people's minds than ever. What I've always thought is that it's not the fact that we all everyone speak differently, and that our accents reflect our backgrounds, but that it matters so much to some people.

Would it be so terribly shocking to admit that the mad variety in our world is a good and interesting thing, not something that should be swept under the carpet? At the Olympics, everyone was terribly excited about the 'melting-pot'. The message was, 'Hurrah, let's celebrate our differences.'

Class seems to be the exception to that rule. Rather

as those faintly sinister 'Eurocrats' in Brussels try to convince us that every nation in Europe should end up being the same (Belgian, I imagine), so people who are anti-class want us all to be as carefully classless as a BBC newsreader.

Why pretend? Am I being dense about this? The only prejudice that really matters is when people believe that one class is better than another. Otherwise, your background is part of you, like your colour, your face, or what you believe.

Between you and me, I feel far more at home talking to one of the gamekeepers at Balmoral or to Annie, who runs the village shop there, than I do in a room of impeccably bred peers of the realm to whom (rather shy-makingly) one is distantly related.

Life is not racing. Bloodlines are unimportant. Sometimes, listening to the conversations of those lucky enough to be born into a certain position and with a certain amount of land, it's tempting to think that too much breeding in humans can be disastrous. Certainly none of them is going to win the human equivalent of the Derby.

Once snobbery is taken away from class, we can all begin to relax a bit – although I must admit this whole area is a bit of a minefield in the family. When we gathered at Christmas last year, Sophie and Edward were explaining to Catherine that certain words and expressions are not expected from us. Catherine asked, with that blush she does so well, if they were referring to 'the T word'!

'Lovey, you mustn't even *think* toilet, let alone say it,' said Teddy Edward.

Catherine seemed worried about these forbidden words, at which point Charles interrupted. 'Snobbery is vulgar,' he said. 'In our position, we should be above such things.'

'Yes,' said Sophie, who's brighter than she looks. 'It's a bit lower-class.'

Poor Charles huffed and puffed until silenced by an unmistakeable rumble, like approaching thunder, from the end of the table where the Consort was sitting.

'Could someone just tell me the words to avoid?' Catherine asked, rather bravely under the circumstances.

At that point, no one could actually think of any words that are, to use the family word, 'doony'. (You'll have heard about doony and non-doony. They're words which I believe came from a flapper girlfriend of Uncle David's, who was obsessed with doing the right thing.)

'One should never call a horse frisky,' Zara managed. 'That's *very* doony.'

Teddy Edward came up with couch and settee, both of which flustered Andrew, who said he had just bought one of each.

'Stroll,' said Sophie.

That caused another silence. Of course, she was right, but why? What is it that makes a walk non-doony, but a stroll doony?

'Anything that's a polite diminutive of the real thing,' said Sophie, who used to be in publicity and makes a study of these things. 'So a wind is a wind, not a breeze. If the sun's out, it's hot, not warm. You do not doze or nap, you sleep. If you're going somewhere, you should never ever pop out, or in or over. A behind is a behind, not a derrière or a sit-upon.'

'Meadow,' said Charles, forgetting his objections for a moment. 'That's ghastly. Why can't people just say field?'

'Jogging's out,' said Andrew. 'And personally, I would never ever dream of going for a ramble.'

'Snacks,' said Sophie to Catherine. 'Snacks are terribly doony. So are nibbles.'

'The jury's out on saplings,' said Charles. 'I'd say a tree is a tree, even if it's small.'

'Hack,' said Zara suddenly. 'When people talk about going for a hack rather than out for a ride, I know they're not really my sort.'

At the far end of the table, the Consort was following this conversation with a grumpy sort of interest. 'I always felt uncomfortable when Rose wittered on about kids. In this family, we have children, I'd tell her.'

That rather took the wind out of the conversation. As you know, Rose (the name some of the staff used for Diana during the difficult times) tends not to be mentioned when Charles or Camilla are present. We all studied our plates for a moment. Before we could change the subject, Camilla, with that natural grace of hers, broke the awkward moment.

'Our nanny always referred to kids,' she said. 'I think kids is absolutely non-doony these days, Philip.'

'Bloomin' kids,' said the Consort, and we all laughed dutifully.

I'm not sure Catherine was any the wiser, but I rather

doubt if she will be popping out for a stroll in the breeze in the near future.

Yours,
ER

Dear Sir Jeremy

I'm sorry if my casual reference to 'Rose' upset you. My letter was written after lunch.

Of course, she is not 'Rose' to me, but Diana. I was always very fond of her and see the period of unhappiness towards the end of her marriage to Charles as one of the worst times of my life.

She had seemed so perfect. Charles had never been terribly good with girlfriends. Unlike Andrew, who's always had that bounderish sense of confidence that girls like (sometimes in spite of themselves), Charles was always a bit of a stick-in-the-mud, romantically. Later, Diana was terribly fond of using the phrase 'self-esteem'. Anything that was going wrong could be explained by so-and-so having 'self-esteem issues'. The one person who was never seen to be suffering from this great modern problem was her husband and yet, I'm almost certain, he was every bit as much of a victim of 'self-esteem issues' as anyone else.

He was terribly awkward as a child, and as an adult. He tried so hard to play the different parts expected of him but was never terribly good at being himself. It has rather haunted me, to tell the truth.

But suddenly, there he was with this beautiful, shy Spencer girl. She seemed so right. Not the brain of Britain by any means, and slightly tongue-tied when we met her, but she seemed fond of Charles in a bashful way and would obviously be popular with the public.

Her age was a good thing, we thought. There's a lot to be said for getting used to public life when one is young, as I once discovered. One gets schooled into it, like a young horse, before bad habits can develop.

Charles was uncertain, but then he had never been the headlong type. We encouraged him to make up his mind. At a certain point in one's life, one is expected to get married, and he had reached that point.

Later, of course, it became clear that the poor chap was all too aware of that. It was time for a wedding. Diana looked and sounded perfect. Everyone thoroughly approved and, almost for the first time in his life, there was a general feeling about the place that he had done rather well for himself. If his heart didn't leap when he saw her, and there was probably not much leaping of hearts on her side, well, that was something they could work on.

In other words, they did the old-fashioned, dutiful thing. They got married because each of them thought it would be good for them, and because it would make everyone else happy. But the old-fashioned thing doesn't work any more. Duty isn't strong enough to hold marriages together. People worry about their own happiness. They see it as a right.

In a way, Diana did grow into the job, but it was her version of the job. After a while, she couldn't care less about what her duties were meant to be, or what was expected of a Princess of Wales. What mattered to her were all the things that are least reliable in the world – the view of the public, emotion, pictures in the newspapers. Of course, the journalists, who couldn't care less about what happened to the monarchy, had a lovely story to work on. There was money to be made.

What chance had a poor little marriage, squeezed between the traditional way of doing things (duty, getting on with what has to be done, even if one's feeling down in the dumps oneself) and the madness of modern fame (being interesting, emotional, sharing one's private life around)? When we saw Charles and Diana, one could tell that the marriage was not exactly going to plan.

He was impatient, she was quiet. That was in the early days. Then, as she appeared more and more in the papers, she grew in confidence. She would tease him, not entirely kindly. She looked bored when he began to expound on the importance of planting trees or of teaching Latin in schools.

There used to be ways around marriage problems in this family. It would be arranged that a couple undertook different duties, which kept them apart. They might, quite discreetly, have their own circle of friends (or more than friends). But that old, civilised way of getting through a difficult patch is no longer an option. The eyes of the press, not to mention the noses of the press, are everywhere. Charles and Diana were trapped. It was utterly miserable.

It all got much worse when Diana began to feel closer to the people on the outside, who wrote to her, and worshipped her from afar (she would actually talk about 'my fans') than to the family and staff who were trying to help her do her job.

All the things that the Consort and I and Charles and our private secretaries and equerries thought were important mattered less to her than the emotion she was whipping up.

At last the people had found a member of the Royal Family who was as vulnerable and warm-hearted as they were.

No one who is a heroine in her own great fairy tale can remain normal. The more Diana talked about her feelings, the more closed-up poor Charles became.

I still wonder whether we could have done more. When they came to stay at Sandringham, I would occasionally see her in the garden, wandering about, a sad, vacant expression on her face as she listened to music through the headphones she took to wearing at all hours of the day.

Once, at lunch, the Consort asked her what the headphones were.

'A Sony Walkman,' she said, rather too brightly. It was a stage when she had taken to referring to things from her own world of fashion and so on without explaining what they were. I suspect she enjoyed seeing the puzzled look on our faces. It gave her a small sense of power, the fact that she was more 'in touch' than we were.

The Consort made a jokily confused face, and thanked Diana, with that light sarcasm he does so well, for making things so clear.

'It's a sort of tape-machine,' Charles explained. 'For pop music.'

Oh dear. How the heart sank. There was a glower across the table from Diana.

'It actually happens to keep me connected to the real world,' she said.

Really more to avoid a scene than anything else, I asked what she meant by the real world. She gave a heavy sigh like a moody teenager.

'Aha, Wham, Duran Duran, Pet Shop Boys,' she said eventually.

I looked at the Consort, who gave a helpless little shrug. Neither of us were any the wiser.

'They're pop groups, Mummy,' said Charles.

'No, Charles,' said Diana with unnecessary sharpness. 'They're talented people who happen to care.' And not for the first time, her eyes filled with tears.

She was a child in many ways. Because she had gone through a beastly time with her parents, she was rather too open to affection. I fear I'm somewhat old-fashioned about that and think it should be earned.

And, as I say, people don't change. Charles remained awkward and tweedy. Diana never quite grew up. We wrote her letters but she was lost. By then there was nothing we could do.

When she died, the first instinct of everyone here, the family, members of the staff – really, everyone – was that the system should take over. This institution has been through wars and death and abdication. When it is being buffeted, the drawbridge goes up. Formality takes over. The traditional processes, the right, formal speech, the correct bit of ceremony, carry us through. The connection to history helps us with the present.

It was the most awful moment when we realised that the reliable, time-honoured approach was no good any more. Everything was upside-down. We used to show the civilian world how to be strong. Now the civilian world was telling us it didn't want strength any more. It wanted feeling. We shouldn't be examples of fortitude at all. We should be more like them.

We were not allowed to have our own private feelings behind the drawbridge. We had to share. It had to be a great emotional final scene, as if we were all part of a cinema film.

Poor Diana. She won. The order of things changed. Some of the old hands at BP became a touch bitter about that and some wag came up with the unkind nickname 'Rose', which somehow, for a while, made discussions of her easier. She became this sad, distant figure, 'England's rose', rather than the slightly confused girl we had once loved.

What times we have lived through, you and I.

Yours,

ER

Dear Sir Jeremy

You are right, as usual. The past, with its dreadful marriage-go-round, has been preying on my mind recently, for obvious reasons.

Although you have never married yourself, I'm sure you can understand just how tricky life in that institution can be. There are few among my married contemporaries who have not been through a phase when the whole thing has become so ropey as to seem hardly worth the bother.

It is usually as the children grow up. Careers are pulling one way, the family the other. Those little habits of the other person, the things they say, are all of a sudden no longer as endearing as once they were. There might be, shall we say, 'distractions' outside the marriage.

We used to put up with it. Things would calm down. The children would grow up and go. The career would begin to seem less important. The distractions would fizzle out, as distractions tend to do.

Then, at some stage of life (in their mid-fifties or sixties) the two people who had been together on this rather bumpy ride would discover, without any discussion, that, however infuriating their husband or wife could be at times, they were still their husband or wife. They were not perfect, heaven knows, but at least they were there, and they were theirs, with shared memories, words, jokes that no one outside the family could understand. There was just, in words that must have been thought, or even said, in millions of marriages around the world, <u>too much to lose</u>.

Although divorce has never been an option for me for obvious reasons, there have been moments in the past when I've sometimes thought about how it would have been to be alone in the middle of one's life, or (a truly dreadful thought) to have to start all over again. Like many women, I'd find the idea of having to train a new man, one who was rather more set in his ways than a younger version of himself, a <u>ghastly</u> idea.

Perhaps I'm out of touch and the new way of doing things has something to recommend it. Modern couples seem to have added a whole new stage to their education in the way things work: first marriage. For them, unhappiness is not something one has to put up with. It's something to learn from.

The idea that this is the person you have chosen before the world and you have a duty to stay together seems to have disappeared.

When Andrew broke the news that he was separating from Sarah (it was a conversation I was becoming used to by then), he used a phrase that has become rather too familiar recently. 'It isn't working.' It was as if his marriage was a piece of machinery that had nothing to do with either him or Sarah. It was like a fridge or a car. It had broken down. It wasn't working. A replacement was needed, one that did work.

People don't change. That's what I've discovered over the years, Sir Jeremy. We get married and think that our presence in the daily life of the other person will somehow make them different, more like us, but it never happens. If anything, as they get older, they become more themselves.

Once people knew that they had to put up with the differences between them. A marriage might be uncomfortable but eventually some sort of equilibrium is achieved.

Now, though, one tends to look for the hairline fracture in a young marriage, the little weakness or flaws that in 10 or 20 years will cause it to fall apart.

Looking back now, I can see the fault-line was there when Anne married poor Mark. He seemed so perfect. Good-looking, an excellent horseman, a decent regiment, and the sweetest smile. Those who serve in the armed forces understand service. They have what the Queen Mother used to call 'bottom'. I thought he would grow into the job, rather as the Consort had all those years ago.

But he was different. He seemed less pleased to be part of the set-up than one might have expected. He was oddly shy for an army officer. I remember watching him at dinner at his first Christmas at Balmoral. The Consort and Anne were in cracking form, and even Charles was making the odd joke.

Mark sat there, a little uneasy smile on his face. When I spoke to him, there was much blushing and mumbling, with not much sense emerging. I noticed a look of irritation crossing Anne's face (she's never been terribly good at hiding her feelings) and I did wonder whether they were quite as happy as one would have expected at that stage.

Some people can manage being part of this family, but most can't. There were times, after I married the Consort, when there would be the most fearful rows between him and that ferocious old Private Secretary Lascelles about what he could or couldn't do or say. Over time, Philip worked out his own way of things. He didn't change, but he did adapt. He didn't allow the role that he had to crush his character. You have to be strong to become part of this family.

With Mark, it was different. Every time I saw him, he seemed less himself – more like a sort of cardboard cut-out than a person. As he became smaller, Anne somehow filled the space that once had been Mark.

It was only when he was riding, circling in a manège or schooling a young horse over some cavalettis that the deadness lifted from his face and he became normal and alive. When Anne told me their 'sad' news (she didn't seem terribly sad, between you and me), I had to pretend to be surprised.

Poor Mark. We hardly meet these days but I have followed his career with interest. Keeping his rank, calling himself 'Captain Mark Phillips' in that slightly vulgar way, rather surprised me. And he has not exactly had a clear round when it comes to his private life. I'm told he has now left his second wife for a girl in her thirties. There was certainly no sign of <u>that</u> kind of behaviour when he was briefly part of the family.

Sarah Ferguson, I always thought, was perfect for Andrew. They seemed genuinely happy in the early days, forever ragging each other in the slightly irritating way of young people who are in love. The fault-line there, I suspect, was not Andrew but what being part of the family did to Sarah.

She was the very opposite of Mark – she liked it all rather too much. Whereas he grew smaller, she filled out. I don't mean physically (she was always what the nannies like to call 'bonny'), but in her personality. Unless you have been raised to understand how it works, as the Consort and I have, there's an almost irresistible temptation to take it personally. The excitement, the interest, the way everyone looks at you and listens to everything you say as if your every word was absolutely fascinating, and laughs at your jokes, however feeble they happen to be. You think it's you. That's human nature. Mark wilted under the attention; Sarah bloomed rather too spectacularly. I remember catching a glimpse of her at Charles's wedding. She seemed to be profoundly moved. There might have been a hint of a tear there but I could tell she was playing a part for the cameras. She was doing what was expected of her, perhaps even trying to draw attention to herself. That's a terribly bad sign.

Then there was the great embarrassment that was Edward's 'Royal Knockout' thing. She looked quite, quite mad. The presence of all those people she had seen on the TV, and the fact that she was at the centre of it all, one of the stars of the show, was simply too much.

I gather that she was so overexcited by the occasion that she brought along a uniform so that she could do a routine with the American who plays Superman in the films. Sarah absolutely insisted that if she dressed up as Superwoman, it would all be terribly funny for TV viewers. I gather she even brought along a script she had written herself.

Teddy Edward agreed to film it but told her later that her scene didn't quite work within the narrative of a medieval joust (he's surprisingly good at this sort of stuff), and so the world was spared the sight of Sarah the Superwoman. I always fear it may emerge in one of those amusing programmes about things that have gone wrong on TV.

The awful thing was that she began to think she was a 'character'. You know how tiresome that can be. At family gatherings, she played the part of the life and soul of the party in a rather heart-sinking way. Now and then she took it into her head to play practical jokes.

On one occasion, while the family were staying at Balmoral, she put that invisible cellophane used in the kitchen over the top of the loo. As luck would have it, Charles was the next visitor. He re-appeared looking <u>very</u> red in the face, with splashes all over his cavalry twills. Hoots of laughter from Sarah, the rest of us thoroughly embarrassed, the Consort looking daggers. Talk about a failure joke.

Andrew's no shrinking violet but even he could see that his wife was taking rather too readily to the business of fame. By then, though, it was too late. She really did believe that it was sweet, bouncing Sarah Ferguson, this funny and fascinating person, a 'breath of fresh air', who was bringing life into the dusty old royal family. Once that starts happening, the marriage will soon be in trouble.

What an awful come-down it must have been for her after the divorce. No longer part of the family in any real sense, she still shows off like mad, but the world pays less attention to her year by year. Like Mark, she tried to live in America for a while. She has done something to do with a diet, I believe, and occasionally pops up on TV, but none of it (like Sarah Superwoman) quite works.

I fear that one of these days, she'll appear on a TV advertisement for dog food or the thing with meerkats. She does <u>love</u> being in front of a camera, and I believe money's a bit tight these days, which comes as no surprise to those of us who know her. She was not the most careful person in the world so far as that was concerned.

My secret wish is that, while the attention shifts to the next generation, Andrew and Sarah will quietly get together again. They are terribly well suited and could grow old together rather happily, spending money, showing off and laughing at the same silly jokes.

We come through these things, Sir Jeremy, or at least most of us do.

When Teddy Edward married Sophie, I found myself wondering what could go wrong this time, and the same has happened with William and Catherine.

But I'm optimistic. Edward learned from his brother and sister. William has seen the misery of divorce and is wiser as a result. I think, generation by generation, we're getting better at the complicated business of men and women.

Yours,

ER

Dear Sir Jeremy

I was amused to read in your latest Bulletin that dear old Mr Prescott, the Labour man who once punched somebody on the nose, has managed to get himself in the news by advising me to retire.

By one of those odd little coincidences, the same thought occurs to me about him when, every few months or so, he pops up in some discussion programme and announces that he is now going to be a policeman (or whatever his latest wheeze happens to be). Good Lord, I think, Mr Prescott is still around. Isn't it about time he retired?

Like many of the Labour politicians, he's a lot more fun than he looks. When they're on parade, these people, being grilled on TV, for example, they behave as if they're terribly fierce and serious-minded. As soon as no one's looking, they relax and couldn't be more charming if they tried.

Harold Wilson was surprisingly twinkly until it became too much for him and he became rather peculiar, and Neil Kinnock is one of the most amusing politicians I ever met, particularly if his nice but slightly dreary wife is not around. Robin Cook, with the ginger beard and rather comical face, was forever talking about hunting (and getting it slightly wrong). Harriet Harman could be delightfully gossipy when she was in the mood, but completely lost her sense of humour in about 2007.

Sometimes I think that the more people present themselves as anti-monarchy, the more they secretly love us. When we visit Australia, for example, the crowds are quite extraordinary, and their sweet, hearty, sun-tanned faces are filled with what I can only describe as love.

Do you remember the fuss when their Prime Minister Keating touched my back all those years ago? It wasn't a lack of respect he was showing (as usual, the papers got it wrong) but simply affection. He couldn't get close enough.

Good, simple people, the Australians. They just can't help expressing their affection, and yet, as soon as our back is turned, they start muttering about how they should become a republic and have their own Australian head of state. It is as if they are almost <u>embarrassed</u> by their own loyalty to the Crown.

Even their current Prime Minister, a socially awkward woman called Gillard (she's Welsh, I believe), was quite overcome and lost for words when we met her. I imagine that, as soon as the cameras are turning, she's a brave republican. That's the way it is 'down under'.

Mr Prescott is rather Australian in that respect. He's very full of himself and bolshie about the family in public but, on the few occasions when we have spoken at receptions, he's clearly thrilled, blushes deeply and has difficulty stringing a coherent sentence together.

I like him, though. The last time I saw him I made a light-hearted reference to croquet (there had been something about his croquet-playing in the newspapers). Off he went, <u>delighted</u> to be able to sound off about what a <u>marvellous</u> game it was, and he was really rather amusing about some of the tricks he plays on the green.

'I hope you don't behave like that in the Labour Party,' I said, preparing to move on.

Quite a tangle of words tumbled out at this point, as if he suddenly thought he had gone too far.

'Maybe we should have a game sometime,' I said. 'The Duke of Edinburgh used to be terribly good at it. Absolutely ruthless.'

Beams of delight from dear Mr Prescott. 'Oh yes,' he said. 'That would be very good, Ma'am. Very, very good, honoured I would be, as it happens, going forward, and the lady wife categorically, too.'

And, as I smiled, he did a little bob, more like a curtsey than a bow, and almost fell over.

You know, I think I prefer the Labour approach to these things to the rather grand air of the Head Boy. If I ever had a game of croquet with him, I suspect he would behave as if I was privileged to be allowed on the same lawn as him.

Yours,

ER

Dear Sir Jeremy

How kind of you to compliment me on my 'star-studded evening'. Apparently, British films are short of money at the moment, and the event to which I was invited was designed to 'raise their profile'.

It was rather fun, I must say. Actors are so full of themselves that they're no trouble when it comes to social occasions. You just wind them up with a question ('What are you appearing in these days?' usually does the trick) and off they go until you move on, leaving them to burble on happily.

I'm still not exactly sure what a 'Bafta' is and why I should be given one, but, whatever it is, it's going straight into the attic. A more hideous object I've rarely seen.

Of course, there was a certain amount of simpering and sucking up, as is usual at 'star-studded' events. People in the acting profession seem to lose the knack of behaving naturally at the first whiff of success. By the time they have reached the top, most of them are quite round the bend.

I asked one of the organisers, Sir Kenneth Branagh (is it my imagination or are there an awful lot of theatrical knights and dames these days?) what my Bafta was for and there were the usual roars of unhelpful laughter. Perhaps it was for my performance, walking down the corridor with James Bond, but that would be odd, since it simply involved playing the part that I've been playing for the last 60 years.

Or maybe it is for giving them material. What would

they have done without us down the years? I couldn't help noticing that the Mirren woman, who has made rather a nice living out of imitating me, was absent, as was Russell Harty, the occasionally amusing northerner who likes to write about me. Or is that Alan Bennett? I get confused.

The Consort tells me Mr Bennett was in a comedy show I saw back in the mists of time called *Beyond the Fringe*. Funnily enough, I do remember a long evening of studenty humour at a London theatre. It was one of those 'shows' where the object was clearly to shock as many people as possible. One of the young men pretended to be Harold Macmillan, I remember, and there was some jokey business about the war, which I confess caused a slight sense of humour failure on my part. No doubt it would be thought completely harmless today, but at that time I was surprised that clever-dick young men were encouraged to be cheeky about people who fought and died for their country. It seemed rather 'cheap'.

Anyway, the amusing northerner went on to be some sort of writer, and popped up years later with a TV play about poor old Anthony Blunt having a conversation with me. I remember being struck by how comprehensively he had grasped the wrong end of the stick when it came to imagining what I was actually like.

It was an odd idea, I thought at the time, to write an entirely made-up story about a person who is still living, but now that there's a small industry of royal writers, I am quite used to it. I suppose the fact that circumstances prevent me from saying what I really think and feel is simply too tempting to resist.

And, of course, virtually every well-known actress, as she reaches, shall we say, 'maturity', has to have a go at playing me. Young men have Hamlet, old men have King Lear, women of a certain age have me.

One thing I've noticed, Sir Jeremy, is that when authors start writing about my family or actors play us, their careers always get a lift. They seem to benefit from the goodwill people have towards us, at second hand.

The Mirren woman is now universally adored. She's become one of the actresses who can say more or less anything in a TV interview (the more risqué the better) and everyone, including the interviewer, falls about with tears in their eyes. Why is that?

And the witty northerner couldn't be more respectable if he tried. Like the Mirren woman, he is routinely referred to as 'a national treasure'.

I wonder if the chippy young man I saw showing off on stage 50 years ago ever imagined that he would end up writing plays about me and becoming a national treasure.

Yours,

ER

Dear Sir Jeremy

Thank you for your characteristically wise Bulletin. You ask, quite rightly, what steps have been taken to prevent Catherine going 'off the rails' in the way of some of her predecessors. She has, as you point out, even less experience of the way we live than Diana or Sarah did.

If you had been at BP over the past year or so, Sir Jeremy, you would have heard much discussion around this very subject. A committee called 'The C Group' has been set up with the specific aim of managing Catherine's image and ensuring she doesn't get in a muddle.

I am imagining your raised eyebrows. You will be thinking rather as I did when I heard about the C Group. We managed without these busy little sub-committees in the old days. Why do we need them now? Does everything these days have to revolve around image and publicity?

Thrusting Justin (this is very much a Thrusting Justin-led idea) explained to me that there is now such pressure from the media and the internet and all the rest that one has to put up what he called a 'firewall'. We need to develop a 'strong narrative' for the press.

I begin to understand. There are so many spinners, publicists and overpaid professional liars out there that one needs one's own team of the same sort of people to do battle with them.

I suggested, rather firmly I must say, that I should attend one of the meetings of the C Group.

It was more interesting than I expected. Clever young men and women sitting around a table with their mobile phones and cappuccinos and skinny lattes in special little plastic containers in front of them (when did coffee get so complicated?). Some of them I knew as members of staff, of course, but several guests were there, too, media experts from universities, a rather amusing former journalist and two or three advertising people.

A pretty young woman did a presentation in front of a screen. I have not the faintest idea of what she was saying (left field, leverage, out of the box and so on) but she showed a rather interesting film of Sarah Ferguson being interviewed on an American TV show, and some clips of Diana and, mysteriously, Princess Michael of Kent.

I think the point the girl was making was that it's a bad idea to allow the press too close to one (top of the class!). At one point, she used a rather striking phrase: 'going native'.

Sarah, I must say, does seem to have gone native in a big way since she started spending time in America. She chatted to the interviewer as if they were old friends, and talked about the sandwiches we would have for tea when she was part of the family (apparently she never liked them), and how I was 'the best granny in the world'. Rather oddly, she referred to me throughout as 'the boss', as if she had read too many articles about me.

I was not going to share my thoughts with a room full of virtual strangers, but I confess I was rather shocked by the fake familiarity of it all. Granny? I'm really not sure I want to be described as 'Granny' in public by my former daughter-in-law. And where did this boss business come from? No one, so far as I know, has ever called me that in the past, and I trust they never will.

The girl doing the presentation said that 'Fergie', as she rather vulgarly called Sarah, had been close to journalists and television for so long that she had begun to see the world in the same way they did, and even (frightful thought) to think like them. The same had happened to Diana and Princess Michael, she said. Those who marry into the family, particularly on the female side, are vulnerable to this pressure. They go native.

So the great plan with Catherine, they all agreed, was to keep the media at a distance. It had been a mistake to encourage the last generation to behave like civilians. Catherine's 'image' should be more carefully controlled. Stories might be leaked about her hobbies (some sport seemed to be a favourite here), and of course she would support the right kind of charities, but there would be nothing too personal, and an absolute minimum of interviews.

Charles's Kitchen Cabinet (you know the one, with Monty Don and Jonathan Dimbleby) had also been considering the matter. We were all given a paper they had produced, which was almost as long as one of Mrs Mantel's articles for the *London Review of Books*. Its conclusion seemed to be that, at some point in the future, Catherine might have a website on which 'she' (that is, a writer commissioned by the C Group) would publish a weekly 'blog'.

At the end of all this, I asked what William and Catherine thought of it all. There were shifty looks around the table and mumbled talk of 'fine tuning' and 'finessing the detail' before a presentation, from which I gathered that the two people most affected had not exactly been closely involved.

I mildly suggested that they should be. I couldn't <u>bear</u> it if at some point stories of the faceless people running the palace emerged. That of course, was exactly what started the trouble with Diana.

Catherine is <u>far too</u> sensible to get in a muddle about these things but I do think Thrusting Justin and his team should be careful about treating her and William as if they were a new 'product' to be put on the market.

Yours,

ER

Dear Sir Jeremy

No, Charles is thoroughly secretive these days about his Kitchen Cabinet. All I know is that once a month people he likes to call 'thought leaders' are invited to Highgrove to discuss matters of great importance.

The internet was one. And something about what's happening to the weather. The press and what to do about it is another favourite topic. God (or not) is a regular.

And, you know, Charles simply is rather cagey about precisely who is invited. I'm sure the long-haired chap with a dinky little beard, Mr Branson, is there sometimes, and Joanna Lumley has become a regular, too. The nicely spoken environmentalist Jonathon Porritt is sometimes there I believe, as is Titchmarsh, the little TV gardener with the annoying smile. Whenever the comedian Stephen Fry is mentioned in conversation, Charles makes a point of referring to him as 'Stephen', and so I imagine he is a 'thought leader', too.

I'm happy that Charles has a project. He's one of those people who likes to have something to worry about (the weather, the economy, the BBC, sparrows, etc., etc.) and for as long as I can remember he has considered himself the family's resident intellectual.

'One has to think these things through,' he says now and then with a slightly befogged look on his face. 'I mean, someone has to, don't they?'

We all solemnly agree that thinking things through is

very important and that he's the person to do it.

Charles's 'egg-heading', as the Consort calls it, started at Cambridge, where he used to have 'think-ins' in his rooms in Great Court. It was the time when the young were slightly hippy and had endless sit-ins and love-ins and be-ins. None of the other 'ins' appealed to Charles but he loves nothing better than to chat airy nonsense, and so a think-in suited him down to the ground.

Apparently, Charles's think-ins became quite famous at Cambridge at one point. Lecturers came to them and authors (no doubt the slightly strange Van der Post was lurking somewhere) and the vicar at Trinity, a chap called Harry Williams, would be there. On one occasion, Jackson, Charles's security chap, reported that a revolutionary was a regular guest. You can imagine how well that went down. And we were right to worry, it later transpired. The youth turned out to be part of something called the Angry Brigade and was sent to prison for putting a bomb on a government minister's doorstep.

After Cambridge, Charles developed the idea that it was part of his role to ponder about things. He was not allowed to have political views or interfere in things, he would say, but he did have a voice and he was jolly well going to use it to talk about important things – how architecture was becoming rather too hideous or why organic farming was terribly important.

I believe the Kitchen Cabinet has been going for several years now. At first, Charles referred to it as 'my little dining club' but when he started casually dropping the names of his diners into the conversation (David Attenborough was an early one, I remember), it became clear that he wanted us to ask questions about it.

One weekend, when he and Camilla were staying with us, the Consort asked him about his dining club, more to make conversation than anything else.

To my surprise, Charles was quite chatty about it. He said he had been reading a lot of French philosophy and he saw himself as an 'outsider' looking into the problems of society. His nickname for his dining club of intellectuals was 'les marginaux', because they were on the margins of the political scene.

I could see the danger signs from the Consort but could do nothing about it. He sort of readjusts himself in his armchair as if it is just about to be launched into space.

'Who exactly are these marginaux, Charles?' he asked, more gruffly than was necessary.

'Michael Palin, Dame Joan Bakewell, Billy Connolly,' said Charles, a touch defensively.

There was a long, rather pensive silence.

'Hm. Marginaux, eh?' The Consort shook his head. 'Now there's a thing.'

I was grateful that he didn't launch an Exocet. Charles is never happier than when he's talking pie-eyed nonsense about thinking the unthinkable and running up flagpoles and kicking things into the long grass. Without ever discussing the matter, we've realised that it would be heartless to discourage him. If producing papers now and then about what's happening to bees keeps him happy, then so be it. He's doing no harm.

'Gosh, you know a lot about stuff, Charles,' Camilla said in her usual tactful way. The Heir Apparent beamed, and I quietly changed the subject before the Consort exploded.

Yours,

ER

D<small>ear</small> Sir Jeremy

How interesting that you went to see the play starring my showbusiness double, Dame Mirren. Nothing surprises when it comes to plays in the West End, but I must say the idea of turning my meetings with prime ministers into an evening's entertainment did strike me as a bit odd.

If only they knew! Apart from Churchill, who was surprisingly 'fruity', to use a favourite word of the Queen Mother's, and Edward Heath, who could be quite interesting about music, they were a dull bunch, at least when they came to see me, either sucking up (Wilson, Blair) or being tricky and defensive (Thatcher, Brown) or simply being old-fashioned crashers (Macmillan, Callaghan, the Head Boy).

You did make me laugh when you wrote about how the feeblest joke or bit of showing-off from one of the actors was greeted by howls of delighted laughter from the audience. On the mercifully rare occasions when I go to the theatre in London, I'm always startled by the behaviour there.

It seems that ordinary people change when they become that mysterious thing, a 'theatregoer'. At the most unfunny line, or some giggling grimace from an actor, they laugh themselves silly. Is it nerves, do you think, or politeness? If there's one thing I find rather wearying in my daily life, it is people pretending to be amused. I only have to say a word ('Really?', 'Goodness', 'Well done') and they're overcome with fake laughter.

When I went to the theatre as a young woman, I worried that I was missing something, or that I had a less well-developed sense of humour than other people. Eventually (I rather think it might have been you who pointed this out years ago) I realised that the audience was performing just like the people on stage. The role of 'theatregoers' is that of people who are tremendously amused or moved, or frightened, by almost anything that happens in a play. They are acting, badly.

I've even been in theatres that are rocked by laughter at one of Shakespeare's 'comedies'. They were some of the longest evenings of my life, I have to say.

It's thought to be terribly important to have a sense of humour, but the truth is most people are only pretending. When Charles went through his Goon phase, he was trying to show the world (and perhaps himself) that he had a jolly, jokey side. It took just a few silly voices in a performance to give him the 'This is Funny' signal, after which he set out to join in the merriment.

The truth is, like me, he tends not to get jokes and, when he attempts to tell one, it's like someone trying to master a foreign language, without much success.

For me to laugh in a theatre, things have to be funnier, not less funny, than in real life. That sweet Tommy Cooper used to manage it at the Royal Variety Shows sometimes, and I had a bit of a soft spot for Les Dawson, particularly when he dressed up as a woman. I know it's unfashionable to say it, but I did think that rude Jim Davidson was funny in his younger days, and so was Billy Connolly before he decided to become all twinkly and respectable. These days,

I'm afraid the Royal Variety Show is a bit of a trial for me.

What I do find amusing, in a quiet, non-laughing way, is how writers and actors try again and again to use characters and situations from my family as 'material', and always – but always – fail.

Dame Mirren makes me too spiky and yet also too sentimental. Actors or comedians impersonating Charles or Diana or Margaret or poor Catherine either do nothing (we really can't be as dreary as some of them make us seem to be) or resort to a sort of cartoon version. The idea that we are really not that extraordinary, that in many ways we are like them, appears not to have occurred.

You'll say that this new play is going to be a hit. Of course. People are fascinated by what goes on in one's life, even if it's a feeble imitation dreamt up by the man in specs or someone else. It's what they call 'money for old rope', Sir Jeremy.

Yours,

ER

Dear Sir Jeremy

I'm grateful for your comments about the question of my being more amusing than many people assume, but I still think that the importance of having a sense of humour is often overrated.

Uncle David was a terrific wag and loved nothing better than to play practical jokes on the staff, asking them to pick up a poker that had just been in the fire and so on, and look what happened to him.

And Andrew was forever playing silly japes at Christmas time, putting plastic dog messes on the carpet, letting off stink bombs in the middle of Christmas lunch. Sometimes I wonder whether it's a way of making up for some inadequacy in one's life.

On one occasion, when Charles was going through his mystical period, reading books on Buddhism and so on, he tried to persuade us all that he could communicate with the dead through those séance things. Andrew, rather naughtily, suggested that the younger members of the family should all have a go one Christmas. I heard from Anne later that they all solemnly sat round one of the tables in the sitting room at Balmoral with their hands on a glass, letter cards all laid out.

When everyone had their eyes closed, Charles (who really did seem to be taking it seriously) murmured an invitation for someone 'out there' to make themselves known.

They were about to give up when Andrew started twitch-
ing and making strangled noises. He said someone who
sounded like Mike was trying to contact him.

Mike? Mike? Who on earth could Mike be?

Then, suddenly, the glass started to move. Sarah
shrieked but was told to keep quiet as the glass moved from
one letter to the next.

Y.I.N.G.

Then it stopped. No one spoke.

Ying? *Ying?*

It started gain.

T.O.

It was at that point that Diana asked Charles the name
of the comedian who used to sing 'Ying tong iddle I po'.

Apparently, Charles went quite pale.

'Not Mike,' he whispered. 'Spike. It's Spike Milligan.'

Andrew, in a spooky voice, said, 'You grovelling little
b——d,' and roared with laughter, followed by Sarah,
Diana, Anne and the rest.

Charles failed to see the funny side and stormed off,
returning to London earlier than planned.

That was Andrew in those days. Always going too far.

On another occasion, he told a 'court correspondent'
that Charles had been meditating with some mystics in
orange robes and had actually managed to levitate several
inches off the ground. The man swallowed it, hook, line
and sinker, and even mentioned it in a book. Charles was
furious.

As you get older, your sense of humour becomes creaky
and unreliable, like the rest of you, and Charles, because

he's always been middle-aged, even when he was at school, has always had to imitate someone who finds things amusing.

I don't know about you, Sir Jeremy, but I rather sympathise with him these days. There's something odd about the need to rag other people at all times. I see that now.

When Uncle David locked one of the footmen in a broom cupboard, or teased the Dapper Monster, a hideous mongrel with a short temper, or made apple-pie beds, it wasn't just to make himself laugh. It may sound silly but there was something <u>angry</u> about it.

You can see it in the eyes of comedians. Behind the smiles and the jokes, there's a sort of rage. Look at Captain Mainwaring in the Consort's favourite programme *Dad's Army*, or the tall, shouting chap in the hotel, or Tony Hancock. I always thought that Charles's favourite funny-man Spike Milligan seemed rather a bitter man.

I've never trusted politicians who are too jokey, either. The laughing Welshman Mr Kinnock could be good company (in small doses) but one wouldn't have trusted him to run the country. Same with that Boris Johnson chap. And that awful little four-letter man Clark.

None of them were quite grown-up. They were thumbing their noses at the teacher, bullying people with their jokes.

I'd be the first to admit that the Consort plays the same game. I hear him, a couple of places behind me, dropping some terrible clanger and causing nervous laughter among his victims, and I just know that he's making a joke because he can and they can't answer back.

I mentioned it to him once, and there was a tremendous harrumphing and what his advisers call 'naval language' (swearing to the rest of us). Bulls-eye, I thought.

Joking is never quite as innocent as it seems.

Yours,

ER

Dear Sir Jeremy

I can't help wondering whether the fuss about poor old Mrs Thatcher has not been ever so slightly 'over the top'?

Of course, she was an extraordinary woman (one of the most extraordinary I have ever met) and she changed everything in a big way during the 1980s, but it seems to me that everyone has gone slightly mad about her death.

Needless to say, dear Huw Edwards was out of the studio, wearing that sombre expression that he keeps for these special occasions. It takes something very important (a bomb, a terrible crash, William and Catherine's wedding) to get Mr Edwards standing outside in the cold, looking concerned.

And the newspapers have dragged up the most desperate piffle to fill up their pages. Mrs Thatcher and sport, Mrs Thatcher and art, Mrs Thatcher and 'the Royals'. On and on it goes.

Briefly, I thought that we could avoid the funeral and send Charles, who loves meeting politicians and having quiet, earnest conversations with them about the great issues of the day. But no. All the usual rules for such things have been cast aside.

The Consort was quickest off the mark, as usual. 'Oh God, it'll be a high-hats-and-medals occasion,' he muttered, as we watched the news on the day she died. 'We're going to have to go.'

'Of course, we won't,' I said. 'There was none of that for Mr Heath. It was all very straightforward.'

The Consort can be the most impossible man sometimes, but I must say, he doesn't miss a trick when it comes to 'trends'.

'Mark my words,' he said. 'Everyone needs parades these days. They had three marvellous do's last year, with the wedding, the Jubilee and the Olympics. This will be the perfect excuse for another one.'

I'm used to Philip's view of the world, but on this occasion I thought he was being unduly cynical.

'It's boredom,' he said. 'These great moments of mass happiness, or sadness, or general excitement, bring everyone together and break up the routine.'

I think I said that, if Mrs Thatcher was bringing the nation together by dying, that would be something of a first, but of course I knew he would turn out to be right as usual. The request came from Downing Street the next day. It would be 'appropriate' if I attended, given Mrs Thatcher's service to the nation.

The view from the press office was that it would play badly if we sent Charles along. As you know better than most, one has rather less power on such occasions than one would like to think.

I fear it's all going to be terribly military. She always considered herself as a great British warrior, a peacetime Mr Churchill, and that's how she will depart. In a strange way prime ministers end up getting the funeral that reflects their personality.

The mousy Mr Attlee had an apologetic little private affair. Poor Mr Heath had an informal, if rather chilly, farewell. I can't remember much about Mr Callaghan or his

funeral. No doubt, when the time comes, the new generation of PMs will get send-offs suitable to their talents. Mr
Major's will be dull and dutiful. The Smiling Salesman's
will be slick and full of fake emotion. The Head Boy's will
be like a school assembly on speech day.

I can't in all honesty say that Mrs Thatcher's funeral
will be one of the more emotional days of my life. I always
found her surprisingly hard work.

All the other prime ministers have at least pretended to
be polite at our weekly meetings. There's a bit of fake
informality, chit-chat about this and that before I get my
weekly report on how wonderfully they've been doing.

She couldn't be bothered. She would bustle in with that
distracted busy-housewife expression on her face, plump
herself down and sound off. As she rattled through the
events of the day, her eyes blazing as if she were being
interviewed on TV by someone who had annoyed her in
some way, I tried to contribute now and then, but was
usually ignored. She had arrived, she wanted to say her
piece and leave. She was a busy woman.

Once I got used to this procedure, I would try to slow
her down, launching a positive barrage of crinklers. How
fascinating you make it all sound. Do go on. Goodness, I
never imagined. In the right tone of voice, any one of these
crinklers can stop a dreary politician mid-flow. With her, it
was as if no one had spoken.

The annual weekend at Balmoral was particularly trying.

I've known people who become huffy and impatient
when they are not working (almost always men) and of
course, as you know too well, there are those who are allergic

to the countryside. Mrs Thatcher was an unattractive combination of the two. Accompanied by her sweet, stunned husband Denis, she would hold forth at lunch and tea, slowing down only when she was given a large whisky and soda at six (even the Consort was impressed by her drinking).

Gradually, as the medicine began to work, the rest of us were able to have a conversation as, not hearing a word, she gazed ahead of her with her dark, infuriated eyes.

Balmoral is a marvellous place and the staff are well trained at putting people at their ease, but during those early visits Mrs Thatcher seemed determined not to be impressed. When we went for an afternoon walk in the gardens, she never actually saw anything. Her whole attention was on herself. She was looking inwards.

Do you know what I think the problem was? I honestly think she was jealous. She was furiously competitive (far worse than any man) and yet I was someone, not that much older than she was, who had a sort of power, who would remain at the centre of things long after she had faded, and who didn't feel the need to compete.

She could never get used to that. In an odd way, she was more chippy about one's position and past and class than any Labour prime minister has been. The fact that nothing at Balmoral had been earned through hard work, and was all inherited, made her frightfully irritable.

Come to think of it, there was one part of the garden which she did notice. The old croquet lawn, just beyond the walled kitchen garden. It had been neglected over the summer before her first visit, and a family of moles was making itself thoroughly at home. Denis Thatcher noticed the mole-holes and, being something of a golfer, harrumphed about the terrible things molehills do to grass.

I mentioned that sometimes one of the little dogs would see the grass moving as a mole made its way down a run and would manage to catch one.

'That's what you must do!' Mrs Thatcher suddenly said. 'Catch them in their runs. Denis, give me that.'

Poor old Mr Thatcher dutifully handed over the shooting stick he was carrying (I think he believed one was meant to take one when walking in the country) and, to my surprise, she began poking the mole-runs with the sharp end of the stick.

I told her that the local mole-catcher would sort it out over the winter months, but throughout the weekend Mrs Thatcher became utterly obsessed by the moles. During quiet moments, she would slip out to the garden with the shooting stick. On one occasion, I looked out from my bedroom window to see the Prime Minister of the United Kingdom on the croquet lawn, stalking about, shooting stick poised, like an old heron looking for fish in the pond. Now and then, she would stab at the ground.

Do you know, she spent hours out there that weekend? What a mercy it was, too. We had much to thank those moles for. Of course, she never got one.

Margaret Thatcher the mole-stabber. That's how I'll be thinking of her as I do my duty at St Paul's.

Yours,

ER

Dear Sir Jeremy

I confess it hadn't occurred to me for a moment that Mrs Thatcher's moley behaviour was peculiar. It was simply her. She had to be in some sort of battle to feel alive.

Of course, we were frightful failures as far as that was concerned. As you know, I can put up with all sorts of nonsense without locking horns (years of training), and the Consort tuned out soon after she arrived. He only enjoys teasing those who are being what he calls (among other things) 'grovellers', and she was certainly not that.

So it had to be the moles. The moles were her President Galtieri (or perhaps Arthur Scargill) for the weekend. Between you and me, the reason why the Consort was unusually quiet over those weekends was that he didn't know quite how to deal with an 'alpha male' who happened to be female. He was too much of a gentleman to send an Exocet back at her, and the other approach he enjoys – good old-fashioned flirting – somehow didn't seem appropriate. He was well and truly stumped when he met Mrs Thatcher and was still unusually quiet for a day or two after her visit.

I read that she became, shall we say, 'vague' during her later years, but I'm sure the mole-stabbing wasn't that at all. It's a thin line between normality and vagueness, and then between vagueness and outright dottiness.

For example, I'm sure that many people (you perhaps) might think it was a sign of 'vagueness' that I can have long conversations with the dogs, and the dogs make some interesting contributions. In my head, of course.

But I've <u>always</u> talked to animals. And is an old lady chatting to a couple of (unusually bright) Corgis any more unusual or odd than a girl talking to her pony, as I would have done 80 years ago? These days I find the dogs (even that ridiculous Labrador, Jake, who hasn't got a brain in his head) rather better company than most humans. Is that a sign of 'vagueness'? Perhaps it is.

Or Peter, the footman. D'you remember him? He was no great age when his behaviour became a slight cause for concern. He had, like a number of staff at BP, originally wanted to be an actor and was always a little, shall we say, 'theatrical'. He liked to make an entrance when serving tea to ourselves and visiting dignitaries. He saw royal life as a show, which I suppose it is in a way.

Suddenly, he started to make slightly peculiar remarks. He would walk in and say, 'Sorry, love. Could I do that again?'

Do it again? *Love*?

Now and then he would look at me with unnerving intensity, and say, 'You know, you're very, very good. I think you're the best lead I've ever worked with.'

One tended to ignore these remarks, and the next day Peter would be his same old self. But a couple of weeks after one such incident, someone rather distinguished (President Suharto, I think) was coming to lunch. We gathered in the library, and Peter came in with sherries, fizzy water and my usual. Halfway through serving them, he stepped back, put the tray down and said loudly, 'Sorry, everyone, I'm going to have to do that again. Can we take it from the top?'

Silence descended on the illustrious company.

'And don't you look at me like that, love,' Peter said to Mrs Suharto. 'I've been doing this since I was at RADA.'

Rather tetchily, he took our glasses back and placed them on his tray. 'I'm never working with these people again,' he muttered at one point.

Luckily, James, the younger footman, was there. As if what was happening was entirely natural, he said to Peter, 'I think the director wants to see you backstage,' and gently led him away.

That was Peter's vagueness. He gradually became convinced that we were all acting in a play. None of it was real. We were rehearsing every day.

You see what I mean by a thin line?

The poor chap is now in a home for retired actors and requires 24-hour supervision but, in a way, he was not that far from the truth.

That was why I wasn't as frightened as perhaps I should have been when that very odd man Fagan appeared in my room out of the blue, and sat on the end of my bed, chatting to me about how I was the only person who could help him.

'You love us all,' he said. 'You're our mummy.'

I've never felt more certain that someone wasn't dangerous. I just listened and made polite remarks, in my usual way.

Obviously, he <u>was</u> insane but then, in the papers just the other day, I read that an eminent actor (that Kingsley chap, he played Gandhi, I think) had told the world that he felt as if I were <u>his</u> mummy, too. His parents hadn't appreciated him and his childhood had been awful in the traditional way of celebrities but, when he was knighted by me, he felt as if he had come home. He said that he wanted to hug strangers in the street and tell them, 'My mum loves me.'

Is that really so different from Peter's delusion? Yet Sir Ben Kingsley is a knight of the realm, talking about it all in an interview, and no one blinks an eye.

Perhaps one shouldn't joke about these things. Everyone took it terribly seriously when official papers revealed, long after he died, that dear Harold Wilson became a little 'out of touch with reality' in the 1970s, although I must say it was no surprise to me. The first time I became aware that there was a problem was when, in the middle of one of our meetings, he suddenly leaned forward in his chair and beckoned me as if he wanted to tell me something in confidence.

'Have you got fillings?' he asked in an urgent whisper.

<u>Fillings</u>? In my <u>teeth</u>?

'Shh!' The Prime Minister looked genuinely frightened. 'Just tell me,' he said.

I said, rather nervously, that I thought I had.

'They're listening to you! The CIA, MI6, they're all working together.' He paused, bewildered eyes gazing into mine, as if he expected me to understand what he was talking about.

'They're tuned in,' he said. 'That's what fillings are for. They let them listen to your thoughts. They send you messages. You have to be very careful what you think.'

He calmed down after I told him that I didn't do much thinking anyway. A few moments later, I accompanied him out of the room to where a member of his private office was waiting.

I was wondering whether I should tell someone about our conversation. It didn't seem a terribly good idea for the country to be run by a man who was convinced that MI6 was sending him messages through the fillings in his teeth.

But the private secretary glanced in my direction and I knew in that moment that he knew, and there was nothing I needed to say.

It seems to me that a bit of confusion is not the most terrible of things, as our poor exhausted brains get older. Life is confusing and the best of us can get in a muddle about things.

Or am I getting confused myself?

Yours,

ER

Dear Sir Jeremy

Yes, thank goodness, this year's birthday passed without too much unnecessary fuss. It seems not so long ago that one simply received a few thousand cards, with the usual polite, badly spelt messages, and perhaps a few hundred paintings from children.

Now there are just a few hundred presents of toys (what are they thinking?), mugs with one's own picture on the front and hundreds – hundreds, Sir Jeremy – of books. I do wonder what people think my days involve. Do they honestly believe that I'm lolling around the library, reading?

It's become quite a thing recently, hasn't it? Reading, I mean. Once books were books. Now they seem to have taken on a sort of magical power to make life better and more fulfilling for everyone.

Children are given books by the government as soon as they are born, poor little things. There are special book days, during which we are all supposed to be reading away like mad. It's almost like a religion, a way of showing that you care, like planting trees.

Not that I've got anything against books personally. When I was young, they were a comfort to me at times when I was really rather on my own. Since Margaret Rose and I never went to school, we didn't know a huge number of children our age whom we could see and play with.

I had the ponies to look after, and the dogs. As I grew up, I began to see that this was how it was going to be, this 'apartness'.

The perfect escape for me was to read. I found the books I wanted on the nursery shelves, and I have some of them to this day. *Moorland Mousie*, the story of an Exmoor pony, I must have read 20 times or so when I was a child. *The Maltese Cat*, about a polo pony, was another favourite, and *The Hill Fox*. At some point, I discovered Ernest Thompson Seton (*Bannertail: The Story of a Grey Squirrel* was one of his – you must have read them) and would devour almost anything by him.

It would be wrong to say that my choices were mostly about animals. They were all about animals. If I thought about it at all (doubtful), I probably assumed that this was what stories were really for. They were to tell us what animals were thinking and feeling, to take us into their world. I <u>loved</u> those books. They were my best friends.

When I was 12, my governess, Miss Crawford, gave me a copy of *Little Dorrit* by Charles Dickens, and told me I would have to write an essay about it when I had finished. It cured me of reading for life.

There was nothing I liked about that book. It was long and had people in it I couldn't care less about, there were no animals, and it kept me, for hour after hour, from doing what I wanted to do – outside with the ponies and the dogs. Once or twice I picked up one of the stories I had enjoyed (the real books, as I thought of them) but even reading them had suddenly lost its pleasure. Miss Crawford said it was time I outgrew them. They were part of my childhood and it was time to read grown-up books.

That, really, was that. Even today, 70 or so years on, I experience a faint but unmistakeable lowering of spirits when I am given an ominously book-shaped present for Christmas.

Teddy Edward is the worst when it comes to trying to convert me. There is always a book 'everyone is talking about'. Last Christmas he gave me a story by the Harry Potter woman, which he said was 'just up my street'.

I told him I was not the slightest bit interested in witches.

'No, no, Mummy,' he said. 'This one's different. It's all about a parish council in a village.'

I experienced a powerful *Little Dorrit* feeling at that moment.

Now Camilla's at it, too. When she became part of the set-up, it was clear that she had to be given a role to keep the newspapers happy. Anything obviously caring (ghastly diseases, starving children, single mothers, the 'differently abled' and so on) would invite comparison with her predecessor (and also, I have to say, made dear Camilla feel a bit impatient).

There were various country charities which would suit her but Thrusting Justin thought that might create an 'image clash' with Charles, who has anything to do with country life 'pretty much wrapped up right now'.

In the end, some bright spark came up with books – no danger of controversy with a book charity, and everyone's in favour of reading. There would be a bit of good work with children, but no tearful scenes. Camilla pointed out that she's not one of life's great readers (she turns out to have read even less than I have, although she's very sound on the Pullein-Thompson pony books). No one seemed to think that mattered too much.

'You won't be tested, darling,' Charles said. 'You just have to wave a few books around and look keen.'

To be fair to her, she's made a tremendous go of it, rushing about the place, handing out books to the bookless, telling everyone how frightfully important reading is, posing as a VIP storyteller with a classroom of goggle-eyed children.

Good for her. There's a lot to be said for someone who just gets on with things without asking too many questions. It's slightly awkward at Christmas if she gets cornered by Teddy Edward when he's in one of his Melvyn Bragg moods and wants to talk about a really rather interesting novel set in a housing estate, which he has just read.

A fixed, slightly panicky smile settles on Camilla's face. I recognise that look all too well. It tells of someone who knows they are in for the long haul.

Mind you, even she gives me books these days. This Christmas it was something called *War Horse*, signed by the author. Rather clever of her, actually, because I remember Uncle David talking about how a hunter of his was one of the few horses taken over to France that actually came back.

It was a ghastly business, and if this new story is as good as Camilla says it is, I might even try it.

Yours,

ER

Dear Sir Jeremy

Yes, what a relief it is that Henry's latest trip to America has passed off without mishap. Ever since he was young it has been clear that so long as he's allowed to rush about and take part in sport and jokes with other chaps, he'll be fine. It's when he's cooped up inside, unable to let off steam in the normal way, that the problems can begin.

His heart is in the right place, and in his way, he is one of the brightest in the family, but he is such a headstrong sort of fellow. He is very much his own person and that can be a mixed blessing in his position.

In many ways, he reminds me of my Uncle David, who was a sweet and rather wild young man until he met the American woman and went round the bend. It's funny how, with every generation, one person comes along who just doesn't quite play the game.

After David, there was Margaret Rose, who loved nothing better than rocking the boat. Andrew was next to play the role, and now it's Henry.

It is as if God wants to remind us every few years how fragile our position can be, in spite of all the fuss and pomp. What happened to poor Margaret Rose, for example, was a living lesson to me, from when she was a naughty teenager to when she was a difficult old woman. If I've managed to set some sort of an example of doing one's duty as a wife, mother and sovereign, she provided a warning. This is what can happen to you if you don't play the game. She misbehaved on behalf of us all, so none of the rest of us had to bother. In a way, and she'd be <u>infuriated</u> to hear it, she was a force for good.

Sometimes, I can see that same spirit in Henry's eyes, even on quite serious State occasions. He has an imp within him, who wants to rag things up. He's a natural tease, always has been, ragging the dogs or ringing up his father and pretending to be Sir David Attenborough wanting to talk about the rainforests. It's his way of keeping boredom at bay.

Of course, being rather wild can be a problem. It's not what is expected. At first, the newspapers like it, but soon they turn. They may say that the Royal Family should be 'in touch with ordinary people', but they don't mean it. When Henry actually does behave like an ordinary person, they're horrified.

If you are not able to cope with boredom, the life that we lead can become impossibly difficult. The way I've explained it to Henry is that every day when I'm at work, I'm in an invisible bubble. Nothing quite reaches me. I'm inside the bubble with my own private thoughts for company. So the endless meetings and conversations which are going on outside the bubble are rather distant. It doesn't matter because no one expects a member of the Family to do more than utter a few vague, polite words and move on.

The bubble is my way of surviving. If it weren't there and I had to have real conversations day in and day out, listening to people's opinions, expressing my own, being happy for them or sharing their sadness, my head would explode after a week!

People hear what they want to hear. They don't want a chatterbox Queen, a sovereign who sounds off her opinions. I say 'Yes', 'Quite', 'How very interesting', 'Oh really' and so on, and they are under the merciful illusion that the two of us have had a conversation. I have understood their situation absolutely perfectly, they think, and have said <u>exactly</u> the right thing.

In the early days, when I was quite young, I'm told I would now and then get things wrong. I'd say 'How marvellous!' when someone was telling me that his wife had died. I would be aware of a slightly startled look on the person's face, but I would just keep smiling and move on. The person I had spoken to would assume that I had misheard, or that he had not made himself clear. No harm would be done.

When it comes to conversation, a process of self-correction takes place. So long as I make the right concerned, interested noises and then move on, I can remain in my bubble and everyone will be happy.

'Doesn't that get a bit dull, Granny?' Henry asked a few years ago. Frankly, that had never occurred to me. I have never seen any problem with dullness. It's a rather useful virtue, in my view.

Compared to dashing Uncle David, my father may possibly have been thought a bit of a plodder. Due to his stammer, he kept conversation to a minimum, never expressed an opinion or made a joke, and perfected the art of gracious small talk. It was partly his character, and partly his choice. He had seen where being interesting and colourful had taken his older brother. Dullness was the coat he chose to wear.

So it is with me. I can see, in every photograph, whether I am in the bubble or not. If someone is impertinent enough to say that I look bored, then so be it. Let them try it for a few days.

I must say, Henry looked a bit down in the mouth when I told him how useful it was to be slightly dreary. Unlike William, who has taken to dullness like a duck to water (I mean that as a compliment), Henry is not very good at going through life with the hand-brake on and the volume down.

I worry about him sometimes. I fear that, to use one of his mother's favourite phrases, his 'life choices' will not always be the wisest.

If he ever found himself in a bubble, he would pop it just for the hell of it.

Yours,

ER

Dear Sir Jeremy

How kind of you to devote so much of your last letter to a sport I know you find rather bewildering. You are right, of course. That moment when my brilliant filly Estimate passed the post in the Gold Cup at Ascot, I was really rather more het up than is strictly appropriate for a person of my position and age!

It was a small miracle that John Warren and I didn't hop about and hug one another. It has been such a long wait, you see. As we made our way down to the winners' enclosure, I found myself thinking of those hours spent discussing which stallion to send our brood mares to, all the setbacks and disappointments both in the breeding and training of our horses, all those people involved at studs and in racing stables, the bloodstock agents, the trainers, the lads and jockeys. No one realises the team that is involved even before a horse gets on to a racecourse.

And we won! It was the most exhilarating moment imaginable, the perfect combination of human and horse achievement, and perfectly timed in this extraordinary year. Even Michael Stoute, not by nature a tearful man, was rather overcome.

I fear I have never quite succeeded in making you see why racing is so important to me, why for me the sweetest, most evocative phrase in the English language is 'They're off!' Horses have been my love and refuge ever since I looked after my ponies 80 years ago. Just being in their presence calms me and puts all the silliness and sadness of the human world into perspective.

One probably shouldn't analyse these things too deeply but, now that I'm getting on and can't even go for a ride these days, I do find myself thinking about what these extraordinary creatures mean to us. For some in the family, admittedly, they have less appeal. Andrew was no horseman and gave up riding at the first opportunity. Edward rode beautifully as a child (he's got the best hands of any of us) but lost interest after he started reading books.

The rest of us have found the area of equestrianism that most suits our character. The Queen Mother loved the mud and thunder of jump racing. For the Consort, it was the excitement of polo, then carriage-driving contests, that appealed. Charles used to love hunting (although, between you and me, he is half the horseman Edward might have been). Anne has always preferred hunter trials and eventing.

For me, it is the flat. The highlights of every year are Ascot, Epsom and Goodwood. I'm never more at ease with the world than when I'm being driven out to the gallops by Michael Stoute to watch one of my three-year-olds working in the early morning.

Racing brings out the best in horses and the best in human beings, too. When people say that class snobbery lives on in the racing world, they don't really understand how it works. There is a sort of social set-up, from the owner to the trainer to the jockey to the stable lad, but it's not about superiority. It's more, I don't know, fitting in with others.

When I visit a yard or go racing, there's less bowing and scraping, and awkward conversations, than anywhere in the outside world. A lad can chat away to me whatever his background because, more important than anything else, we share this love of the same thing. I'm told that you can see it on my face when I go racing, and I imagine that's true. At Sandown or Kempton, I can forget who I am and enjoy seeing these extraordinary animals doing what they have been bred to do.

As I get older, memories of the famous people I have met (the prime ministers, the equerries, the showbusiness 'personalities') begin to fade, but I remember every one of my horses, from Aureole all those years ago to my gallant Estimate. A poem by George Whyte-Melville sums up my feelings better than I ever could. I used to know it by heart and I can still remember the last verse. It goes:

> I have lived my life, I am nearly done,
> I have played the game all around,
> But I freely admit that the best of my fun
> I owe to horse and hound.

See you in the winners' enclosure, Sir Jeremy!

Yours,

ER

Dear Sir Jeremy

I was, of course, on the edge of my seat like everyone else. It was a wonderful victory, and something of a relief after all those years and years without a Wimbledon men's champion. At least we can relax a bit now, and perhaps spend rather less time watching people we've never heard of grunting and punching the air on a tennis court. I've always thought Wimbledon was a rather useful excuse for people who enjoy sitting on their backsides for hours while pretending they are actually doing something – a bit like fishing but indoors.

Well done, Andy Murray, I say. There was something cheeringly old-fashioned about the way he played. It was as if he knew that being a great British sportsman in front of a great British crowd, he simply could not lose. We seem to have lost that ruthlessness in recent years. Lester Piggott had it, and so did Harvey Smith. Maybe a few motor-racing drivers or cricketers had it many years ago.

Henry tells me that our footballers are of the opposite inclination. As soon as the nation wills them to win, they get into a terrible state and fall apart. Quite why that should be I have no idea. I confess that football is something of a closed book to me.

I was impressed by the grown-up way Mr Murray handled his interviews. No blubbing, praise the Lord, and a certain generosity towards his opponent. It's interesting how sportsmen can mature over time, isn't it? A few years ago, Mr Beckham could hardly string two words together if the TV cameras were running. Now he's smoothness itself.

Politicians, on the other hand, seem to be going in the opposite direction. In the presence of their sporting heroes, they gawp and gurgle like starstruck teenagers. I suppose they think it makes them look more 'in touch with ordinary people'.

I mean, did you see the Head Boy when Mr Murray appeared in Downing Street the day after the game? He actually bounded out of the door with a mad smile on his face, rubbing his hands.

Whatever happened to the dignity of office, Sir Jeremy? I can't remember feeling as embarrassed by a senior politician since the Smiling Salesman bounced a football on his head ('head tennis', is it called?) with some professional footballer or other. Back and forward the balls went with Mr Blair crouching down and darting about like a schoolboy showing off to his parents.

What a fool he looked. I can't help feeling that, when he later had to meet great world leaders to discuss issues of global importance, their first thought will have been, 'Isn't that the silly ass who likes to bounce a football on his head?' It really can't have helped his case.

Did I imagine it, or did Mr Cameron make a particularly ill-judged remark about Mr Murray deserving a knighthood – as if honours were little more than another trophy that get handed out after a victory? To his credit, the tennis-player, when asked about this, replied with more dignity than the Head Boy could manage.

The prime ministers of the past may not have been quite as bright as today's lot (d'you remember that sweet old Douglas-Home?) but at least they didn't pretend to be sportsmen.

Yours

ER

Dear Sir Jeremy

It is, as you so rightly say, a moment to remember. Your Bulletin paints a marvellous picture of the general brouhaha, but I must say that all seems like a distant clamour to me. To the world, little George may be a future king, but to me he's just a very sweet great-grandson.

Yes, we have met. I am not, as you know, a baby person. It's only when they start to speak and develop their own little personalities that I can truly warm to them. That soft, pink, vulnerable creature is something to be wondered at, but one couldn't exactly feel warmth towards it – relief, wonder, all those things, but anything else has to be earned.

This time, though, was oddly different. You know, I felt really quite tearful! That little thing, what a life it has in front of it. I thought of all those other Georges down the centuries – kings and yet all too human. What a weight of history this new George already has on his tiny little shoulders.

No doubt, one day he will be able to look back and say, 'I knew old Queen Elizabeth, you know,' and everyone will be amazed, rather as I was when my father told me how he used to sit on Queen Victoria's knee.

It worries me that he is at the back of a long queue. There's me, then dear, patient Charles, then William. It will seem like an eternity of waiting for poor George. Maybe he won't mind.

Looking at his sweet little face (we do produce good-looking babies in this family, I must say), I found myself wondering about what the future holds for all of us.

For me, I sense, it will be about the family – this brave, battered family and the dogs and the horses, and what's growing in the gardens. Those are the things that these days seem really rather more important than another visit full of smiles and awkwardness, another polite conversation with someone I shall never see again.

Of course, I shall stay. Much as I envy Beatrix her freedom in Holland, I shall keep going in the way that everyone expects of me. The finishing-post is not that far away. It would be rather feeble of me to do a Devon Loch at this stage.

It's odd, being a great-grandmother. The years have made one a bit more distant from the children than used to be the case. I remember enjoying playing with William and Henry when they came along (rather more than I had with their father, uncles and aunts, if the truth be known), but this time around, it's somehow not expected of one.

To my surprise, I find that I simply can't wait for George to be old enough for me to be able to have a great-grand-motherly chat with him. The things I'll tell him!

How he should enjoy his childhood, because in those years he will be as private a person as he will ever be.

How the family matters above all else (and how I wish I had known that 60 years ago).

How it's wonderful to be carried along by the love of millions of people but that he should remember it's not unconditional. He should try to be the person they expect him to be, at least in public. Otherwise they will feel oddly betrayed and can so easily turn.

How he should have animals near him throughout his life. There was a word his late grandmother Diana sometimes used – 'grounded'. I always rather liked that. The very best way to be 'grounded' is to have a few dogs to look after, or perhaps have a brood mare or two.

How he should spend as much time in the country as possible. There is less of the madness of modern life there.

How there's really a lot to be said for cultivating the appearance of dullness. It's when people in the public eye try to be interesting and original that the trouble begins.

How he should never ever be interviewed, particularly by a Dimbleby (there will always be a Dimbleby around).

How the way to avoid going round the bend is to divide yourself into a public you – a person going about his duties, being discussed in the newspapers – and the real you. These days, when I read the latest newspaper chat about myself, I'm really quite interested. 'Now what's she been up to?' I think.

How he should believe in something beyond this world of ours, some great and distant Uncle, and keep that belief to herself like a secret treasure.

How he should follow his heart, not what is expected of him, when it comes to finding a wife. How, if he's very lucky, he will find a female, 21st-century version of the Consort (no, I can't imagine that either).

How, in the beginning and at the end, we are just little humans trying to do our best during our brief second in history. There's not as much difference between us and the people watching and waving flags at us as the chattering world would have us believe.

How, when he becomes a busy public person, he should seek to find someone to guide him through his daily duties who is as similar in every way as is possible to his great-grandmother's dear, wise, loyal Sir Jeremy.

Yours,

ER